Fred McKenzie

Sober by act of Parliament

Fred McKenzie

Sober by act of Parliament

ISBN/EAN: 9783337151935

Printed in Europe, USA, Canada, Australia, Japan

Cover: Foto ©Suzi / pixelio.de

More available books at **www.hansebooks.com**

SOBER

BY ACT OF PARLIAMENT

BY

FRED A. MCKENZIE

LONDON

SWAN SONNENSCHEIN & Co., Ltd.

NEW YORK: CHARLES SCRIBNER'S SONS

1896

TO

THE MEMORY OF

MY FATHER,

WHO,

THOUGH PASSED FROM HUMAN KEN,

HAS LEFT BEHIND

A PRECIOUS REMEMBRANCE OF LOVING KINDNESS AND

UNFAILING SYMPATHY,

This Book is Dedicated.

PREFACE.

It is a truism that men of all shades of opinion are desirous to promote sobriety. It is the *raison d'être* of the teetotaler and the declared aim of the publican. The advocate of prohibition and the man who would make the trade in drink as free as the sale of bread both profess to be actuated by a desire to extirpate inebriety. Can legislation aid us in accomplishing this end, and if so in what way and to what extent? This volume is an attempt to partly answer the question, not by means of elaborate theories or finely drawn inferences, but by a statement of the actual results obtained from liquor laws in various parts of the world.

Whatever shortcomings may be found in the following pages, I have done my best to ensure their honesty and fairness. I have written with a brief for no particular policy, but with a sincere desire to learn, free from the blinding mists of partisan prejudice, the truth about all. My conclusions may appear to some mistaken, and my treatment inadequate, but I have never suppressed facts that told against my own opinions, arranged statistics to suit myself, or consciously placed incidents in a disproportionate light. The subject is altogether too serious, and involves issues too grave, to allow one to indulge in one-sided statements, garbled facts, or lying statistics.

As far as possible, the facts and figures given are taken from official sources. I must acknowledge my indebtedness to many correspondents in America, in Australia, and on the Continent of Europe, as well as at home, who have helped me by collecting statistics and supplying information. Without their aid my investigations would have been far more difficult than they have proved. I am also greatly obliged to the Editor of the *Pall Mall Gazette* for permission to reproduce portions of several articles of mine on " Liquor Laws," which appeared in his journal and in a *Pall Mall Gazette* " Extra " during 1893.

FRED A. McKENZIE.

46 OXBERRY AVENUE,
FULHAM.

CONTENTS.

PART I.—AMERICA.

CHAPTER   PAGE
I. The State as Saloon Keeper - - - - - 9
II. Rum and Politics - - - - - - - 21
III. Forty Years of Prohibition - - - - - 32
IV. Prohibition in Kansas - - - - - - 45
V. The Law that Failed - - - - - - 53
VI. High Licence in Pennsylvania - - - - 67

PART II.—GREATER BRITAIN.

I. Prohibition and Local Option in Canada - - 75
II. Local Control in New Zealand - - - - 92
III. Licensing in Australia - - - - - - 104

PART III.—THE CONTINENT OF EUROPE.

I. The State as Distiller - - - - - - 112
II. The Gothenburg System - - - - - 122

PART IV.—ENGLAND.

I. The Growth of the Licensing System - - 133
II. Proposed Reforms - - - - - - - 147
III. The Problems of Reform - - - - - 169
IV. The Path of Progress - - - - - - 191

APPENDICES.

I. The Condition of Working Men in Maine - - 199
II. The Gin Act, 1736 - - - - - - - 200

SOBER BY ACT OF PARLIAMENT.

PART I.

AMERICA.

CHAPTER I.

THE STATE AS SALOON KEEPER.

DURING the last few months South Carolina has been the scene of a remarkable experiment in liquor legislation, which has attracted considerable attention from social reformers everywhere. Though professedly based on the Gothenburg system, the Dispensaries Act differs from its prototype in many important respects. As in Sweden, the element of individual profit is eliminated, and the control of the trade is taken out of the hands of private persons ; but in place of the drink shops being conducted by the municipalities, they are placed under the direct supervision of the State Government. The saloon has been abolished, and its place taken by dispensaries, where liquor can only be obtained in bottles for consumption off the premises. All public inducements to tippling have been removed at a sweep; and while it is possible for any sober adult to obtain what liquor he wishes, no one is pecuniarily interested in forcing intoxicants on him. The Act was in operation for too short a time to allow anything definite to be said as to its success or failure. It received the fiercest opposition from an influential body of politicians, and from the more lawless section of the community; and the dispossessed saloon keepers, with all the following they could command, naturally did their best to cause it to fail.

In the election of 1892 the prohibition party showed great activity, and succeeded in obtaining a majority at the polls. The question of the control of the liquor traffic occupied a foremost place at the meeting of the new Legislature. Many members were in favour of out-and-out prohibition, and a Bill was introduced to make the manufacture or sale of drink illegal. But, after considerable debate on the subject, a new measure was hastily brought before the Senate, at the instigation of the Governor, the Hon. Benjamin R. Tillman, as a compromise between the views of the extreme prohibitionists and those who held that, in the present condition of public opinion, prohibition would be largely inoperative, and consequently injurious to the temperance cause. The measure was rushed through the Legislature with little or no debate, and at once received the sanction of the Governor.

Governor Tillman is undoubtedly a remarkable man,

of bold initiative and great force of character; and it is impossible to understand the situation in South Carolina without knowing something about him. Within the last decade he has risen from obscurity to the supreme power in the State, and to-day he is "boss" of South Carolina. He first came to the front in 1885, by his bitter denunciations of the local Democratic rulers. He is himself a Democrat, but this did not prevent him from bringing the most serious charges against the members of the aristocratic ring that held the reins of Government. He charged them with being the enemies of the poor and oppressors of the people, whose one aim was to conduct public affairs so as to benefit themselves. At first the high-class politicians treated him with a half-amused, half-contemptuous scorn, sneered at what they were pleased to call his ignorant talk, and held his language up to ridicule. And in truth, if reports may be believed, his vigour of speech gave his enemies abundant cause to blaspheme. He was not particular in his choice of phrases, and he did not hesitate to pile up the most picturesque and sanguinary expressions in describing his opponents.

But the people rallied around him. " I am rough and uncouth, but before Almighty God I am honest," he said to them ; and they believed him. The poorer country folks were his first followers, then the Farmers' Alliance came to his support, and before the old politicians had ceased to wonder at the audacity of the young man, they began to learn that their days of power were over. In 1890 he stood for the Governorship in opposition to the regular Democratic candidate. He stumped the State, and met with a most enthusiastic reception. He was elected by a large majority, and the power of the old ring was, for a time at least, broken. Two years later he was once more elected to the same post, and until he tried to carry out the Dispensaries Act his authority was supreme in the State. One thing is certain : if Governor Tillman cannot secure obedience to the law, it will be difficult to find any one else who can.

The chief provisions of the original dispensary law are as follows. No persons or associations of persons were allowed to make, bring into the State, buy or sell any intoxicating liquors, except as provided for by the Act. Districts that were previously under prohibition continued so, but in other parts the traffic was conducted by State-appointed officials. The Governor appointed a Commissioner, whom he must believe to be an abstainer from intoxicants ; and this official, under the supervision of the State Board of Control, purchased all strong drink to be sold in the State, and generally acted as head of the dispensaries. The State Board appointed in each county a local Board of Control, composed of three persons believed not to be addicted to the use of intoxicants. These County Boards made the rules for the sale of drink in their own districts, subject to the approval of the State Board ; and they also appointed dispensers who had the sole power of selling liquors in the districts where they were placed.

There are many minute restrictions which had to be

observed by the dispensers in vending their wares. A would-be buyer must make a request in writing, stating the date, his age and residence, and the quantity and kind of liquor required. If the applicant was intoxicated, or if the dispenser knew him to be a minor or in the habit of using strong drink to excess, then he must refuse to supply him. If the dispenser did not know the applicant personally, then a guarantee must be given by some person known to both buyer and seller that the former was neither under age nor a habitual drunkard. Sales were only to be made during daytime, and the liquor was not to be drunk on the premises.

The penalties for breaches of the law were very severe, ranging as high as imprisonment for not under one year or over two years for repeated illegal sales. All profits obtained by the work of the dispensary were divided in three parts,—one half for the State, one quarter for the municipality, and one quarter for the county. The hope of obtaining a considerable revenue was undoubtedly one of the main reasons for passing the Act, and Governor Tillman anticipated a profit of half a million dollars a year for the State.

The dispensers were paid, not according to the quantity of their sales, but at a fixed salary named by the Board, and not allowed to exceed a certain amount. It was provided in the original Act that dispensaries could only be opened in cities and towns, and then not unless the majority of the citizens of a place signed a petition requesting to have them.

The new measure came into force on 1st July, 1893. For many weeks previously there had been great excitement in the State, and as June drew to an end the saloon keepers put forth strenuous efforts to do the utmost possible business in the short time that was left to them. "The situation all over South Carolina to-night," said a despatch from Charleston on 30th June, "is peculiar. In Charleston there has been in progress all day a huge whisky fair. The air is filled with the tintinnabulation of the auction bells and with the cries of the auctioneer; in dozens of liquor stores are crowds of free-born American citizens buying whisky, wine and beer to lay in a stock against the dry spell, which sets in to-night. In the fashionable groceries extra forces of clerks have been at work day and night for a week, putting up demi-johns and kegs of whisky, brandy, rum, gin, and wine; and battalions of drays and delivery waggons have been employed carting the goods to the railroad depôts and to the various residences. It is no exaggeration to say that there are not 1000 out of the 10,000 houses of white people in the city that are not provided with a supply of liquors to last six months at least."

Six counties in the State are under statutory prohibition, and consequently no dispensaries could be opened in them. In many other parts the people refused to come under the Act, and in towns especially there was a spirit of undisguised opposition to the measure. It is in the towns that the old-line Democrats, whom Tillman drove from office, have always been the strongest. With the passing of the Act they saw their opportunity to have vengeance on him, and possibly to regain their old majority; and they resolved to do their best to wreck his Bill. In Charleston the word went forth that the law was to be ignored, and, as far as the city authorities could accomplish that end, it has been set at defiance. When the State constables have arrested liquor sellers, the constables have been mobbed and ill-treated; the sheriff has packed the juries; the justices who have tried liquor cases have been notoriously opposed to the law; and, as an inevitable consequence, the clearest evidence of illegal liquor selling has been insufficient to convict any offender there. What is true of Charleston is almost equally true of several other places. This, it must be understood, is not because of any fault of the Act; but because eager partisans are willing to perjure themselves, to break through the most sacred obligations of office, and to descend to any tricks in order to ruin the Tillmanites.

The prohibitionists have been divided in their attitude. Some of them warmly support the law, but others have united with the old-line Democrats in opposing it. They are mostly willing to admit that the Tillmanite dispensaries are a vast improvement over the former reign of the saloon; but they are fearful lest the fact that the State conducts the traffic may give it a semblance of respectability, encourage people to drink, and so do more harm than good.

"The absolute boss of the State, Governor Tillman," sneered one, "expects to turn the great commonwealth into one great drinking saloon, such as might carry a signboard, reaching from sea to the mountains, announcing 'Benjamin Ryan Tillman, monopolist of grog'."

In his annual message to the Legislature, in November, 1893, the Governor gave a long and detailed account of the working of the law. According to this statement, there were then fifty dispensaries open, and the total sales in the four months had amounted to 166,043 dollars, 56 c., yielding a profit to the State of 32,198 dollars, 16 c. This was considerably less than had been anticipated ; and the smallness of the profit is no doubt due to the facts that so many people had got in their supplies of drink before the Act came in force, and that in many parts the law was very imperfectly enforced. Since the Governor issued his report there was a very considerable proportionate increase in the gains.

In order to ascertain the results of the law on intemperance a circular was sent out to seventy-five cities and towns, asking them to state the number of arrests for drunkenness and disorder arising from liquor drinking for a like period before and since the passing of the Act. Only thirty-three places replied; and in the whole of these the arrests from 1st July to 30th Sept., 1892, under the old licence laws, were 577 ; during the same period in 1893, under the Dispensaries Act, the arrests were only 287. In September, 1892, 231 arrests were made ; in September, 1893, the arrests were 131.

The Governor admitted that the amount of illegal liquor-selling going on in the State was considerable, and for this he blamed the local authorities and the railway companies. "There is hardly a train entering the State," he declared, "day or night, passenger or freight, which does not haul contraband liquor. Some of the railroads are yielding a measure of obedience to the law ; but most of them openly defy it, or lend their line to smuggling liquor into the State. . . . The police in the cities, as a rule, stand by and see the ordinances broken every day, are *particeps criminis* in the offence, or active aiders and abettors of the men who break it." In order to stop these things, and to more efficiently enforce the law, the Governor demanded fresh legislation.

In answer to this demand, the State Legislature passed a new measure in December, giving considerably increased powers to the executive. The State Board of Control was authorised to deprive any city or town refusing to actively co-operate in the enforcement of the law, of its share of the dispensary profits. In place of the Board being unable to open a dispensary anywhere except when a majority of the people petitioned for it, the law was made that the Board could establish its shops wherever it pleased, unless a majority of the people petitioned against them. It was also found advisable to modify several minor points, such as giving hotel keepers permission to serve their guests with liquor.

Governor Tillman at once made full use of the new powers. He announced that several new dispensaries

2

would be opened in different parts, and he sent a circular
to all the mayors, asking if they intended to assist the
State officials or not.   To those who answered in the
negative, he at once sent notice that the share of the
profits for their towns would be withheld from them, and
used for the purpose of employing special constables to
see that the law was carried out there.

In March, 1894, the troubles created by the opponents
of the Dispensaries Act came to a head.   Some State
constables were searching for contraband liquors at Darlington when the people rose in arms against them.
Two constables and two townsmen were killed, and the
police hastily retired to a swamp. Here they were pursued
by an infuriated body of citizens ; and, had they been
found, they would unquestionably have been killed.
For a day or two, matters wore a serious look.   In one
place a dispensary was gutted, and several bodies of
the State militia, when ordered by the Governor to proceed against the rioters, refused to obey.

Governor Tillman is not a man to be easily intimidated.
He promptly seized the telegraphs and the railways, prevented as far as possible the rioters communicating with
sympathisers in other parts, and called together the
troops he could rely upon.   "As Governor I have sworn
that the laws shall be respected until they are repealed,"
he said, addressing the militia.   "So help me God, I
will exert all my power to enforce them.   Although some
of the militia have refused to obey orders, there are still
enough to obey.   The opponents of the law must submit

to the rule of the majority. My life has been threatened ;
but I have no fear, and I will convoke the Legislature if
further power is necessary." The soldiers received his
message with enthusiasm. At the same time the Federal
authorities offered to send a large body of national
troops, should they be required, to quell the rioting,
and in a few hours the powers of the law and order were
once more supreme. But had Tillman been a ruler of
another stamp, had he shown the least sign of yielding
to the disaffected, or of eagerness to compromise, then
the outbreak at Darlington would probably have been
only the beginning of serious trouble in the Palmetto
State.

Hardly, however, had the riot been suppressed before
the State Supreme Court declared the Act unconstitu-
tional. The court, which consists of two conservative
judges and one Tillmanite, based its decision on the
grounds that the measure was not a prohibitory law
and was not a police regulation, but was solely a
plan for giving the profits of a trade to the State, and
therefore it conflicted with the lawful rights of the old
saloon keepers. Justice Pope, the Tillmanite, dissented
from this view, and pronounced in favour of its being
legal, but he was out-voted by his brother judges.

The result of this decision is, that all the State dispensaries have been closed, and the saloons are now
again openly conducting their business. It is hard to
say what the final outcome will be ; for the people in the
country parts declare themselves resolutely determined

not to have the saloon system revived. It is said that as soon as possible one of the old judges will be removed, and his place taken by a Tillmanite. The measure will again be carried through the Legislature, and once more come before the Supreme Court. The court will then uphold it, and the State will give the Act another trial. But, even if this is so, the prospects of the scheme cannot be said to be bright. There are now enlisted against it a powerful political faction and the authorities of several municipalities. It can count on the unceasing opposition of many whose support is almost absolutely necessary to its success ; and hence it will be more than a wonder if, while thus handicapped, it can be anything but a failure.

CHAPTER II.

RUM AND POLITICS.

AMERICA is pre-eminently the land of legislative experiments; and it has unequalled facilities for giving trial, with comparatively little risk, to many of the professed solutions of those problems which the artificial life of civilised society has produced. On nothing has it made more numerous or varied experiments than on efforts to promote sobriety by law. Each State in the Union is free, within certain limits, to regulate or suppress the liquor traffic within its own borders, without interference from the Federal Government. The latter body, however, maintains freedom of inter-State traffic, and has the power to tax liquor, and to impose internal revenue fees on brewers and saloon keepers. These fees are most strictly enforced; and the first thing a man does who contemplates entering the drink trade, whether legally or illegally, is to take out his internal revenue licence. Even the individual who surreptitiously sells half a dozen bottles of whisky a month in the lowest "speak-easy" rarely thinks of attempting to evade the Federal revenue law; for conviction is so sure, and the penalties are so heavy, that it does not pay.

In seeking to learn what lessons can be taught to old-

world politicians from the new-world experiments, it
must be borne in mind that, although the Americans are
mostly of one blood with ourselves, the conditions of
their social and political life are yet very different. The
liquor problem occupies a far more prominent place
there than at home, and the saloon keeper is an influential force in State, Union, and City politics. The temperance element is strong and active, and exercises a social
influence not easy to estimate. A solid public sentiment
has been created against even the moderate use of intoxicants; personal abstinence is advocated as part of the
routine in nearly all the public elementary schools; it is
regarded as disreputable for a man to frequent saloons;
and, except under very extraordinary circumstances, no
respectable woman would think of crossing their door-
steps. Many employers of labour, especially railway
companies, go so far as to insist that their hands shall
be abstainers. But while the work of the teetotalers
has been productive of much socially, their political work
has been far more spasmodic, and less effective. They
are split into cliques; and whatever proposal may be
brought forward, there is almost certain to be a body of
irreconcilables who fight against it. In America, as in
other countries, the greatest opponents of temperance
legislation are always temperance reformers: if a law is
moderate, then it incurs the enmity of those who believe
that any other plan than the utter and immediate destruction of the saloon is sin; if it satisfies the extremists, it
is opposed by those who declare that such uncompromis-

ing legislation will produce a reaction, and so in the end do more harm than good. A still greater cause of weakness than even their internal divisions is the temporary character of much of their work. The respectable people of a city or State will rouse themselves to a fever-heat of emotion over some social reform, and will carry it into law with a rush. Then the excitement will gradually die away, and in a shorter or a longer time the new law will be left to enforce itself; affairs will soon drop back into their old groove, until, possibly, some time after, a specially flagrant case of law-breaking again arouses the public conscience, and the same thing is gone through once more.

The brewers and saloon keepers work differently. They are efficiently organised, and have behind them an almost unlimited supply of money and a considerable voting power. Their work is not the unselfish advancement of some general benefit, but the protection of their own pecuniary interests. They have shown themselves willing to sink all partisan preferences in order to prevent their trade being extinguished, and they have attempted to save themselves by securing control of the political machinery. They have too largely succeeded. America, in spite of its unceasing boasts of liberty, is especially the land where the few dominate over the many. In industry, the rings and monopolies rule; in politics, the "bosses" are supreme. The people are allowed to retain in their hands all the paraphernalia of political authority; but in many parts they are ruled by autocratic political organisations, with saloon keepers and plunderers of the public at their head.

It would not be just to pronounce the same sweeping condemnation on politicians in all parts of the Union alike. In most country parts and in some cities the government is all that could be desired; and, usually, the more native-born Americans and English and Scottish settlers there are, the more free are the officials from corruption. But in many cities the administration is absolutely rotten : the courts dole out injustice, the municipal officers solely study their own interests, and obtain office for the one purpose of dishonestly acquiring public money; laws are enforced or set at defiance as may be most profitable ; and perjury and plunder are the every-day business of mayors, aldermen, policemen, and justices alike. The plunderers are elected to office mainly by the saloon vote, a large proportion are or have been drink sellers themselves, and for these things the saloons are largely responsible. It is the realisation of this that has induced many men, by no means ardent abstainers, to advocate prohibition, not so much because it prevents intemperance, but because it breaks the power of the saloon in politics.

The source of the power of the saloon lies mainly in three things: (1) The absorption of respectable citizens in their private concerns, and their indifference to politics; (2) the political machines; (3) manhood suffrage.

On the first cause but little need be said. In America

the race for wealth is keener than anywhere else; the almighty dollar is worshipped, and most men are in a hurry to make their piles before the end of next week. A large proportion of the business men allow themselves time for nothing but money making, and those who have leisure regard politics as disreputable. In England our best citizens are glad to serve the commonwealth at their own cost; in America, a rich and cultured man would in many cities be looked upon by his friends as either a crank or a boodler if he announced his intention of adopting a political career.

On the subject of manhood suffrage generally and its desirability or otherwise, I have no intention of entering in this place. But coming to the result of manhood suffrage on American politics, few can doubt that it has exercised in some ways a most evil effect. If all the citizens to whom the ballot has been given were intelligent and educated, and knew anything of the politics of the country which they are helping to rule, then suffrage would be robbed of much of its evil effects. But at present the peasant who has been picked from the wilds of Connemara, the lazzaroni from Naples and Rome, the offscourings of the slums of the cities of Central Europe, are able to out-vote in many towns the genuine Americans. They are brought under the influence of ambitious and unscrupulous political organisers almost as soon as they land at New York, and too often their ballot papers are cast solid for the maintenance of fraud, falsehood and robbery.

The results of machine voting, the rule of the "bosses" and saloon politics can perhaps best be seen in one well-known instance. The city of New York, the metropolis of America, has actually been controlled for some years, not by its inhabitants, but by an ex-drink seller, Richard Croker, and his subordinates. This man was originally a young rough, in due course he developed into a saloon keeper, and after a time he resigned his bar for the more profitable employment of politician. He now holds no office under Government, he has no ostensible means of earning a living ; yet he is able to maintain a magnificent country mansion and a town palace ; he owns as fine a team of trotting horses as most men in the State ; and he is well known to be enormously wealthy. His horses are said to be worth seventy-four thousand dollars, and he owns a half interest in a stud farm valued at a quarter of a million. When he travels the railway companies provide specially luxuriant cars for his special accommodation, and he receives such homage and abject worship as exceed the subservience shown by the poorest-spirited courtiers to any petty princeling. Over his long-distance telephone he controls local politicians and the State Legislature, and he can wreck Bills or bring them into law almost as he pleases.

The secret of Croker's power is the fact that he is the head of Tammany Hall, the most powerful political machine in the Union. Under this body, New York is mapped out into about eleven hundred electoral districts, each containing a few hundred voters, with a "captain," who is usually a saloon keeper, over each. It is the duty of the "captain" to get as many people as possible in his district to join Tammany, and to vote on the Tammany ticket; and woe to him if he lets the Hall lose power there! He has innumerable methods of attracting voters to himself. Any man who has a little local influence is instantly noticed, and has tempting visions of place and power held out before him if he will only consent to throw his lot in with the party. The Tammanyite who is in trouble with the police knows that he can obtain the friendly services of the "captain" to speak a kind word for him to the justice; and it is wonderful how far these kind words go with the politically-appointed justices. The Tammanyite who is out of work will naturally look to the "captain" to help him to something, whether it is a clerkship in the municipal offices, a street-sweepership, or a higher and better paid post. The "captain" may or may not be paid openly for his services; but he receives plenty of either direct or indirect emolument. If he is a saloon keeper, numbers of people naturally flock about his place, and deal of him. He is a man of weight, to be respected as such!

No party organisation like this could be held together without powerful motive forces. To some of the Tammany "captains" need not be denied purity and honesty of aims; but it is to be feared that such are in the

minority. Tammany as it is conducted to-day rests on
bribery, swindling and corruption. Those whom it can
buy, and who are worth buying, it buys, whether they
are senators or street-sweepers ; those who are not to be
bought, it often terrifies into passiveness. If a public-
spirited citizen shows himself inclined to kick hard against
his lawful rulers, and if he is a person who can be safely
annoyed, then the municipality lets him feel the weight
of its wrath.   It does not use the old-time methods
of casting him into prison, cutting off his head, or the
like ; for such crude expedients might attract an un-
pleasant amount of public attention.   The recalcitrant
citizen to-day has the assessment of his property for the
purpose of taxation increased to perhaps double its former
amount ; city officials suddenly discover that his house
transgresses some local ordinance, and order him to make
costly structural alterations.   If he is a saloon keeper the
power of the "boss" over him is almost unlimited, and
the unlucky wight can be hauled up before the justices
almost every week, and fined or imprisoned continually.
Hence few saloon keepers dare to offend.   There are
a thousand and one ways in which Tammany can punish
its opponents.

But if Tammany is cruel to its foes, it can be very kind
to its friends.   The happy man who does it service finds
money, place, and power waiting him.   The saloon keeper
can defy the Sunday closing law with impunity, and the
business man has his house assessed very moderately.
The young fellow of talent who throws his lot in with the

party knows that in due course (when he has earned his reward) he can be almost certain of a comfortable competence in a municipal or Government post. Tammany has no less than twenty-seven thousand rewards, in the shape of municipal offices, to distribute among its friends.

On first hearing of these things it seems inexplicable to an Englishman why the honest people of the American metropolis do not rise up and destroy such an institution. The reasons are manifold. It must be remembered that even Tammany is not all bad. Among those who blindly follow its ticket are many who believe that they show their patriotism by doing so. The "boss" is backed by a political party; he is a Democrat, and many upright Democrats think that this fact alone compels them to throw all their influence on the side of the man who carries their party colours. Moreover any party of reform has to reckon with the thirty thousand votes of the city drink sellers and their men, which are cast solid for Tammany so long as it helps them. Without the saloon and its help, Tammany would not keep together for twelve months; but with its influence on its side, it is no easy task to overcome it. To-day the churches are struggling, the newspapers are denouncing, leagues and societies are being formed against the common enemy; yet Tammany still rules. Last autumn a majority was elected to the State Legislature against Croker's party, and it was confidently expected that at last its power would be curtailed. By the peculiar system of controlling New York city,

the State Legislature has considerable power of interfering with its affairs. Accordingly, this year measures
have been brought forward that would have done great
damage to Croker's friends. But even this session
sufficient senators have been found willing to break
through their solemn electoral pledges, to vote against
their own party, and to wreck Bill after Bill directed
against the municipal ring. The Tammany men openly
proclaim that they can kill every other reform in the
same way. No secret is made of the reason for the
senators' change of face. It is openly said in conversa-
tion, and plainly printed in the papers, that they were
bribed by Croker's agents.

It may be asked where Croker and his men get the
necessary money from to carry on their work. The
answer lies in one word—blackmail ! Business men are
politely requested to contribute to the funds of the Hall,
and if they refuse they are looked upon as enemies, and
treated accordingly. Every man who is allowed to break
the law, whether he is a saloon keeper who keeps a side
door open on Sunday, the owner of a gambling hell, or
a more respectable sinner, is expected to allow a solid
cash consideration for the privilege. If any one or any
corporation wants a favour of the local authorities, the
only way of obtaining it is to grease the itching palms
of the aldermen, and to make friends with the politicians.
Even those who want perfectly legitimate permits granted
to them from the city can only get what they need by
paying heavily for them. " All the laws good and bad,"

said Mr. Kelly of New York recently, "are so mis-executed by Tammany as to give it a clutch upon busi-ness men and especially the liquor dealers. . . . The power of the ring seems to depend upon its power to play upon the hopes and fears of our citizens."

The result of Tammany rule on New York city has been indescribably bad. Notorious law-breakers have been appointed to the most responsible posts, either because they had done some service to Tammany, or because they were willing to pay the highest price for the appointments. Justices have been put in office, not because of their learning or integrity, but because they are willing to twist the laws to suit Tammany. Even the electoral returns have been fraudulently altered to place the nominees of the Hall in office.

It is impossible in one short chapter to give any elab-orate details of the extent to which corruption prevails in American cities ; but enough has been said to show that the conditions under which temperance reformers have to work there are very different to those that prevail at home. The difficulties are greater, the means for enforcement are less effective, and the powers of lawless-ness are more potent.

CHAPTER III.

FROM the time of the earliest English settlers in America the drink traffic has been looked upon as a business requiring special regulation. The influence of Puritan immigrants in the middle of the seventeenth century led to the framing of many severe liquor laws. Ludlow's Connecticut Code in 1650 dealt with the subject on the basis that "while there is a need for houses of common entertainment . . . yet because there are so many abuses of that lawful liberty . . . there is also need of strict laws to regulate such an employment"; and it was enacted "that no drink seller should suffer any person to consume more than half a pint at a time, or to tipple more than half an hour at a stretch, or after nine o'clock at night". The first American prohibitory law was passed by the English Parliament in 1735, when " the importation of rum or brandies" in Georgia was forbidden. This was done at the instance of James Oglethorpe, then head of the colony, who declared that the excessive sickness there was solely due to the over-consumption of rum punch.

While Oglethorpe remained at Savannah the law was strictly enforced, and all spirits found were destroyed;

but after he left it was allowed to fall into abeyance, and in 1742 it was formally repealed by Parliament.

The modern legislative movement took its rise between 1830 and 1840, when the whole of New England was convulsed by an uncompromising campaign against intemperance. Almost the entire community seemed for a time carried away by the crusade against intoxicants. In nearly every place powerful temperance societies were formed; many gin merchants closed their distilleries, and saloon keepers put up their shutters and bade the people come and spill the contents of their rum barrels down the gutters. At first, teetotalers relied solely on moral suasion; but soon the more advanced section in Massachusetts and Maine demanded that the law should aid them by putting a stop to the legalised sale of drink. As early as 1837 a committee of the Maine Legislature on licensing laws reported that "the traffic (in strong drink) is attended with the most appalling evils to the community. . . . It is an unmitigated evil. . . . Your committee are not only of opinion that the law giving the right to sell ardent spirits should be repealed, but that a law should be passed to *prohibit* the traffic in them, except so far as the arts or the practice of medicine may be concerned." At that time the traffic in intoxicants in Maine was considerable; but the saloon keepers were without any efficient organisation, and consequently could not offer any united opposition to the new movement. There were seven distilleries, and between three and four hundred rum shops in Portland alone. Ac-

cording to the Hon. Woodbury Davis, ex-Judge of the
Supreme Court of the United States, "nearly every
tavern in country and in city had its bar ; at almost every
village and 'corner' was a grog shop, and in most places
of that kind more than one. . . . Men helplessly drunk
in the streets and by the wayside was a common sight ;
and at elections and other public gatherings there were
scenes of debauchery and riot enough to make one
ashamed of his race."

It is often stated that before the passing of prohibitory
legislation Maine was one of the poorest and most deeply
indebted States in the Union. This is true, but it is not
the whole truth. Maine had not long been separated from
Massachusetts, and its Legislature, maybe partly intoxicated by its newly acquired powers, ventured on some
expensive undertakings. A few costly public buildings
were erected, and a premium of eight cents a bushel was
offered to farmers on all wheat or corn over fifty bushels
that they raised in a year. The consequence was that
the heavy taxes proved altogether insufficient to meet the
expenditure, and by early in the forties a State debt had
been incurred, equal to three dollars a head of the population. Money was very scarce, and both the local government and private individuals were glad to borrow wherever
they could. But in spite of the scarcity of money, Maine
was not generally regarded as poor. It took the first place
in the Union as a shipbuilding State, and the second in the
coasting and fishery trades. "The prosperity of Maine,"
wrote a skilled financial observer in 1847, "was never

greater than at this moment. . . . She will become one
of the first States of the Union." Ten years earlier, in his
Annual Address to the Legislature, the Governor said: "It
affords me great pleasure on this occasion to be able
to speak of the prosperous condition of the State. . . .
The State, as well as our citizens individually, are rich in
lands, in timber, in granite and lime quarries, in water
power for manufacturing purposes, and, to an equal extent
at least, with any other State in the Union, in all the
essentials of profitable industry except monied capital."

Neal Dow, the son of a rich Quaker farmer, travelled
from village to village in Maine, urging the people to rise
up against the legalised sale of the drink ; and, largely in
consequence of his agitation, a tentative Prohibition Act
was passed in 1846. The first Act was a complete failure ; it only dealt with ardent spirits, and did not provide
adequate means for suppressing the traffic in them. Five
years later, Mr. Dow, then Mayor of Portland, framed a
more comprehensive measure, and had it rushed through
the State Legislature in a couple of days. When the
people understood what the new Bill meant, its provisions
excited a great deal of opposition. Rioting took place in
several towns, and was only put down by calling out the
militia. In one of these riots a lad was killed, and this
so strengthened the pro-liquor party that in 1857 the Act
was repealed; but it was re-carried the following year, and
it has ever since been in force. A final step was taken
in 1884, when an amendment to the Constitution was
submitted to direct popular vote, providing that the sale

of liquors be for ever prohibited. Seventy thousand electors voted for it and only 23,000 against, so the alteration was made. The consequence of this is that the sale of drink can now only become legalised in Maine by two-thirds of the electors voting directly for it.

For many years the one aim of the temperance party has been to make the prohibition law as effective as possible, and to secure its enforcement throughout the State. Wherever any clause in it has been found unworkable it has been quickly altered, and every possible legal device has been used to ensure the destruction of the drink traffic. The manufacture, sale, or keeping for sale of intoxicating liquors as a beverage is absolutely prohibited. Any person illegally selling, attempting to sell or assisting to sell is liable, on a first conviction, to a fine of fifty dollars, and imprisonment for thirty days, and to increasing penalties for subsequent convictions, the maximum imprisonment being two years. It is considered sufficient to convict if a person pays the United States internal revenue liquor tax, issues a notice offering to sell, or delivers to another any liquor. Liberal powers of search are given to the authorities, and all liquor found by them is destroyed by spilling on the ground. Municipal officers are compelled to take action on having their attention drawn to any cases of supposed law breaking; and thirty taxpayers in any county can, on petition, obtain the appointment of special constables to secure the better enforcement of the law. The necessary sale of spirits for medical, mechanical and manufacturing purposes is made by specially nominated agents, who are supposed to obtain no profit by such sales, but to be paid a reasonable remuneration by the municipalities appointing them.

In considering the working of this law, it must be remembered that Maine presents almost as favourable a situation as could be asked in order to give prohibition a fair trial. It is isolated, and has no towns of any size. Its citizens are mostly native born Americans, farmers and fishermen, innately religious and law-abiding. The foreign element, which presents so disturbing a factor in many parts, is almost a negligable quantity here. In 1850 there was a population of 583,169, of whom only 31,825 were foreigners. Nearly three-quarters of the people were engaged in agriculture, about one-tenth were mariners, and another tenth found employment in connection with the trade in timber. Apart from saw-mills, all the factories together did not employ above two or three thousand men. Since then factories have greatly increased, and a number of French Canadians and Irish have settled in the State. But Maine is still principally an agricultural district, and its largest city to-day contains less than forty thousand people.

After a trial of forty years, has prohibition proved a success or a failure in Maine? The answer to this question entirely depends on the point of view from which one looks at the subject. In so far as it has not entirely destroyed the drink traffic, prohibition is not a success; but it has succeeded in diminishing crime, pauperism and drunkenness, and in greatly increasing the wealth of the people. In 1857, a few years after the law came into force, there were only eleven savings banks in the State, with 5000 depositors, and a total of deposits and accrued profits of about a million dollars. In 1882 there were fifty-five savings banks, with 90,000 depositors; and the Hon. J. G. Blaine estimated the aggregate deposits and accrued profits at 30,000,000 dollars or more.

Pauperism has shown a steady decrease. From 1860 to 1870, in spite of an increase in most of the neighbouring States, the number of recipients of official charity was diminished by 21.4 per cent.; from 1870 to 1880, there was a further diminution of 11.6 per cent. ; and from 1880 to 1890, notwithstanding the fact that the increase for the whole of the States was 10 per cent., there was still further reduction in Maine of over 20 per cent. In 1890 the number of paupers was 1161, or only about one-sixth per cent. of the population. The significance of these figures is increased when it is remembered that Maine is an old settled State, and in such the number of pensioners of public charity is usually far greater than in newly opened up districts. Insanity, on the other hand, has spread during the last thirty years by leaps and bounds. From 1860 to 1870 the number of insane in the State increased by 12.5 per cent. ; from 1870 to 1880, the increase was 94.7 per cent. ; and although the complete figures for the last

decade are not yet published, there is every reason to
believe that they will be no more favourable. At first
this seems to show that there must be some mysterious
connection between teetotalism and madness; but further
investigation reveals the fact that this increase has not
been confined to Maine alone. In seven other North
Atlantic States, where liquor selling is permitted, the
increase has been far greater : during the first period it
was 48·8 per cent., and during the latter 138·4 per cent.
The voluminous statistics on divorce supplied by the
Government Bureau on Labour[1] do not tell conclusively
either one way or another as to the influence of the
law on married life; for divorce laws differ so greatly in
various States as to make comparisons practically valueless. In Maine there are abundant facilities for undoing
the marriage tie ; consequently, the number of divorces
granted is decidedly over the average for the whole of the
country : though in some States, where divorce is even
easier than in Maine, such as Illinois, the proportion
is far greater than there.

Crime is steadily on the decrease, and the average
number of criminals in Maine is lower than in any other
State in the Union. The number of convicts in the
State Prison is now less than in any time for twenty-seven
years; in 1890 there were 65 convicts; in 1891, 50; in 1892,
34. The total number of commitments to the county

[1] *A Report on Marriage and Divorce in the United States*, by
Carroll D. Wright, Commission of Labour. Revised edition, Washington, 1891.

gaols for all crimes (including offences against the drink laws) is also on the decrease, as is shown by the fact that in 1890 there were 3780; in 1891, 3665; and in 1892, 3515 commitments.

The official returns of the value of property cannot be altogether relied upon ; for it is a notorious fact that real estate is systematically under-estimated for the purpose of taxation.　But while giving no accurate idea of the value of the holdings in the State, they do show that the material prosperity of Maine has greatly increased.　In 1857 the valuation of property was about a hundred million dollars; according to the annual report of the State Board of Assessors for 1893 the valuation was 270,812,782 dollars.　The Census Department estimated the true valuation of real estate in Maine in 1890 at 254,069,559 dollars.

It is admitted on all sides that the prohibition law has not succeeded in entirely extirpating drinking, and liquor can still be obtained in most of the larger cities by those who seek for it.　But the open bar has been almost everywhere swept away ; and those who wish for liquor have either to order their supplies from other States or else go to work secretly to obtain them.　The prohibitionists claim rightly that they have put the traffic outside the sanction of the law, and have made it "a sneaking fugitive, like counterfeiting—not dead, but disgraced, and so shorn of power".　The returns of the Department of Internal Revenue show that there are still a considerable number of drink sellers in

Maine. In 1890 there were 868 retail dealers in liquors of all kinds, and 73 retail dealers in malt liquors. During the fiscal year ending 30th June, 1892, there were 808 retail and 7 wholesale liquor dealers, and 214 retail and 5 wholesale dealers in malt liquors. There were no brewers or rectifiers. It must be remembered that every person licensed under the Maine law to sell drink for " medicinal, manufacturing, or mechanical purposes " is reckoned in the Government returns as a liquor dealer; and that the individual who at any time sells a single glass of rum is at once made to pay the tax by the revenue officials, and tabulated by them as a licensed liquor dealer for that year. So although there are nominally 808 retail dealers, it would be a mistake to suppose that there are 808 saloons doing business in Maine. Considerably over half the total criminal convictions are connected with breaches of Prohibition Acts. The number of committals for liquor selling and drunkenness in 1890 was 2300; in 1891, 1468; and in 1892, 1714.[1] The divorce statistics also show that drunkenness has not been entirely suppressed; for in the twenty years ending in 1886, 432 divorces were granted for habitual intoxication, either alone or coupled with neglect to provide.

[1] Mr. C. W. Jones, Inspector of Prisons and Gaols, Maine, to whom I am indebted for these figures, adds that the increase in commitments in recent years " is not because those crimes are on the increase, but because of the better enforcement of our laws relating to those crimes ".

Yet, there has undoubtedly been an immense reduction in the consumption of drink. One who should be a most excellent authority on the question, the Revenue Superintendent of a portion of the North Atlantic States, said early in 1872 : " I have become thoroughly acquainted with the state and the extent of liquor traffic in Maine, and I have no hesitation in saying that the beer trade is not more than one per cent. of what I remember it to have been, and the trade in distilled liquors is not more than ten per cent. of what it was formerly ". The latest available revenue returns show that the drink trade has been further reduced to about one-eighth of what it was at the time this was said. The same revenue returns give the most conclusive proof possible of the great reductions in the traffic. In 1866, when prohibition was only very partly enforced, Maine paid 2,822,000 dollars in internal revenue, chiefly on drink and tobacco ; in 1887 the amount paid was only 50,000 dollars, or less than two per cent. of its former amount.[1]

The drinking that now goes on may be divided into three classes,—(1) open violations of the law, (2) secret drinking, and (3) obtaining liquor from the authorised city agencies. The open violations prevail now to a very slight extent; but for a long time three or four cities, especially Portland, Lewiston and Bangor, practically set

---

[1] *The Report of Commissioner of Internal Revenue*, pp. 314-319. Washington, 1892. There are no returns available for any year after 1887, as since then Maine has ceased to be reckoned as a separate district for revenue purposes.

the law at defiance. The authorities let it be understood that they would not take action, and juries refused to convict even on the clearest evidence. This was partly due to personal feeling, partly to political considerations, and chiefly to the fact that the rum sellers were strong enough to turn out of office either Republicans or Democrats, did they attempt to proceed against them.

Most of the drinking that goes on is done either secretly or through the licensed vendors. Of the secret drinking it is not necessary to say much; for it no more proves the uselessness of prohibition than the existence of illicit stills in Scotland and Ireland proves the impracticableness of our licensing system.

The selling by the city agencies is a far more serious matter. These places are supposed only to sell drink for the purposes allowed by law; but, as a matter of fact, they are often little better than saloons licensed to supply spirits to be consumed off the premises. People who are well known to require liquor solely as a beverage can obtain it with ease on simply stating that they want it as medicine or for trade purposes. Judging from the amount of whisky sold as medicine in Portland, a considerable proportion of the inhabitants of that place must be chronic invalids.

Yet in spite of its failings, the people of Maine regard their law as a success, and mean to maintain it. As a correspondent, himself a State official, and in a good position to gauge public opinion on the question, recently wrote to me: " In the discharge of my official duties I frequently visit all the cities of Maine, and in no parts of the country do I see fewer cases of intoxication than in Maine cities and towns. In our country towns a rum shop or a drunken man can rarely be found, where formerly liquors were sold at every store. Our people are prosperous, and an overwhelming majority of them are perfectly satisfied with our Maine liquor laws."

CHAPTER IV.

PROHIBITION IN KANSAS.

ALL things considered, Kansas is one of the most successful instances of State prohibition in the Union. The conditions of life there are very different to those that prevail in Maine, and the liquor law has had to be enforced under many disadvantageous conditions. Kansas is a Western State, nearly half as large again as England and Wales, and with a population of less than a million and a half. Like many other parts of the far West, it was for some time the refuge of disorderly elements of Europe and the Eastern States; and even now there is a very considerable "cowboy" class which makes the carrying out of restrictive legislation extra difficult. None of its cities contain over forty thousand people, and the number of foreigners in the State (excepting English families) is comparatively small. It has a large boundary line, and is bordered on three sides by States in which the drink traffic is legalised.

In 1880 a prohibitory amendment to the Constitution was proposed and carried by a very small majority; and the following year saw the passage through the Legislature of a measure to give enforcement to the amendment. This was only done after a very fierce fight, and for a time the opposition was so strong that it was found practically impossible to give effect to the law in many parts. In 1882 the friends of prohibition were heavily defeated in the State elections, and it seemed as though the Act would certainly be repealed. But there came a reaction in favour of temperance; and in place of repeal, the original statutes were in 1885 considerably strengthened. Since then public feeling has been growing stronger yearly in favour of the perpetual ostracism of the liquor traffic.

According to the law as it at present stands, the penalty for keeping a saloon is a fine of from one hundred to three hundred dollars and imprisonment from thirty to ninety days. If the person who obtains the liquor is intoxicated by it, then the seller will be held responsible for any harm he may do while in that state; and his wife, child, parent, guardian or employer may bring an action against the seller for injury done to them through being deprived of means of support, etc., and obtain exemplary damages.

The chief difference between the Kansas law and that of Maine is that the sale of drink for purposes other than tippling is made through licensed druggists, instead of through city agencies. The regulations to prevent the druggists from selling drink for other than medical, manu- facturing and mechanical purposes are very strict. No druggist can trade in alcohol without a permit; and he can then supply only on an affidavit of the customer, de- claring the kind and quantity of liquor required, the purpose for which it is wanted, that it is not intended to be used as a beverage, and that the purchaser is over

twenty-one years old. Any person making a false affidavit
for liquor is counted guilty of perjury, and is liable to imprisonment from six months to two years.

The affidavits have to be made on properly printed
and numbered forms, supplied by the county clerk,
and have to be sent in once a month by the druggist
to the probate judge, with a sworn declaration that such
liquor as stated has been supplied in due accordance with
the law. The druggist has also to keep a daily record,
in a book open for inspection, of all drink sold. For
breaking these regulations he is liable to a fine of from
100 to 500 dollars, and imprisonment from thirty to ninety
days, besides losing his permit. There are still further
checks and affidavits required, in the hope of making
drug store tippling impossible. But these have by no
means succeeded in their purpose. They have led to a
considerable amount of perjury ; and both druggists and
customers have developed such elastic consciences that
most of them will now swear affidavits to any extent
required.

In Kansas the prohibition question has been made a
partisan one. The amendment was carried irrespective
of politics; but when the Legislature had to frame the laws
the Republicans declared themselves strongly in favour of
active enforcement ; and, after the usual manner of politicians, the Democrats took up the other side. Up to a
few months ago, to use the local parlance, "in the platform of the Republican party there was always a stout
prohibition plank," and the party never met without

making a declaration in favour of thorough enforcement. Every Republican was a defender of the law ; and it was repeatedly said that much of the drinking in cities was mainly due to the wilful slackness of the Democrats who had control of them. But at the last State election there came a change. The Republicans have for some time been supreme in the State; but recently there has arisen a new party, the Populists, which has attracted great numbers of the farmers from the older political bodies. In Kansas the Populist movement is specially strong, and in the last election, by a combination of Populists and Democrats, a Populist Governor was elected, and the Republicans driven from office. The present Populist majority, while not so pronounced on prohibition as were the Republicans, still expresses its firm intention of maintaining the law. The Republicans now, somewhat disheartened by their defeat, are inclined to hedge on the question. Their leaders declare that they will no longer bring forward a resolution in favour of enforcement at their conventions, but will instead state in their programme that "the Republican party is, as it always has been, the party of law, and in favour of enforcing all laws on the statute book". They say they will do this because it is now wholly unnecessary to specially declare in favour of one law more than another; but there is no doubt that the real reason is the hope of being able to draw to their side a number of hesitating pro-liquor voters, and so win back their old position. One of the leading Republicans of the State, the Hon. John R. Burton, frankly explained the state of affairs when he said: " It is high time the Republican party of Kansas quits its foolishness, and if it expects to succeed it must go before the people on strictly political issues. It is time to quit riding a hobby, and next year we must make up our platform without any relation to the isms."

But while the party leaders, sore after their defeat at the polls, may talk like this, there is very little likelihood of their proposing or supporting any retrograde movement ; for to do so would be to court certain disaster at the elections. The great body of the people are enthusiastically in favour of the law, and even many of those who grumble at it would join together to prevent the re-enactment of licence in the State. Religious and temperance organisations abound, and are active in compelling the officials to resolutely enforce the law.

Prohibition is now fairly carried out in the whole of the State, with the exception of Wichita, Leavenworth, Atchison, Kansas City, and Fort Scott. In these places the law is almost a dead letter, and drink can easily be obtained, though the saloons do not openly advertise their business. Yet, even after allowing for them, it cannot be denied that the law has led to a very considerable diminution in the consumption of liquor, and, with it, a decrease in the rowdyism which was once rampant. The number of persons paying the Inland Revenue tax has, it is true, increased within the last few years, but this is no test of the amount of the intoxicants used. The returns, prepared by the United States brewers them-

selves for trade purposes, of the number of barrels of
beer consumed within the State in six recent years are as
follows :—

1887	...	...	...	...	...	16,488
1888	...	...	...	..	...	15,285
1889	...	...	...	...	...	9,700
1890	...	...	...	...	...	2,700
1891	...	...	...	...	...	2,050
1892	...	...	...	...	...	1,643

The amount derived by the central Government from
Inland Revenue taxes has also shown a considerable
decrease, though not nearly so great as the above.

Innumerable statistics have been brought forward by
those favourable to the law, to prove that it has had a
most beneficial effect on the social and moral condition
of the people. But it is an open question how far the
small amount of poverty in the State and the reduction
of crime are due to prohibition. I have no wish to
minimise the actual good accomplished by the law, but
it can serve no useful end to claim for it benefits that are
produced by other causes. Kansas is a new settlement,
and its surroundings and circumstances are such that
we might naturally expect its people to be comparatively
free from poverty and its allied evils. The problems that
menace the older civilisation of the East, over-crowding,
starvation wages, and lack of employment, are hardly felt
there, and it is not fair to claim as the outcome of one
law the results that are due to many causes. The greatest
benefits of prohibition in Kansas are of another kind,

impossible to show by arrays of figures, but none the less real for that. The rising generation is free from those temptations which wreck so many of our own youth. The man who is a wilful drunkard can, no doubt, find out where to obtain liquor; but he who is weak rather than wicked does not have alcohol flaunted in his face wherever he goes. A strong public sentiment against excess is created; and those who are doing battle with the liquor traffic naturally find themselves opposed to the allied evils of gambling and impurity. Hence, in the greater part of Kansas, the social evil is kept under, gambling dens are unknown, and the whisky ring is banished from politics.

One charge has repeatedly been brought against the law in this State—that it has checked the inflow of population. "The hour that ushered in prohibition," said the Hon. David Overmyer, Democratic candidate for the Governorship, in a speech at Salina last December, "closed our gates to the hardy immigrant, the home-seeker, the strong and sturdy class that develops a country. . . . It has driven law-abiding and enter-prising citizens from the State." Statistics certainly show a decrease in the population within the last few years. There was a great inflow of immigrants from 1870 to 1880, and from 1880 to 1888 there was a further increase of the population of from less than a million to over a million and a half. But from 1888 to 1890 there was a decrease of about ninety thousand, thus reducing the increase in the ten years to about 43 per cent. Since 1890 the number of inhabitants has probably been stationary. The decrease in recent years, however, has been due, not to any State law, but principally to the fact that great tracts of Indian territory immediately below Kansas have been opened up to white men, and there has been a rush to them. When the reduction is allowed for, Kansas showed a greater increase in population from 1880 to 1890 than many of the principal Western States in which drinking is licensed.

CHAPTER V.

THE LAW THAT FAILED.

THE commonplace truth that, under representative Government, restrictive legislation can only succeed so far as it is backed up by the hearty support of the great majority of the people, has recently received a striking illustration in Iowa. Twelve years ago the people of this State voted, by a majority of 29,759 out of 280,000 votes, in favour of an amendment to the Constitution making the sale of intoxicants for ever illegal. Owing to some flaw in the method of taking the vote, the amendment was subsequently declared by the courts invalid; but in 1884 the State Legislature carried, and for a long time the authorities in most parts have tried to enforce, what is probably the most drastic measure of prohibition known. Everything possible has been done to make the conviction of liquor sellers sure; the law has been so drawn, even in the opinion of many in favour of restriction, as almost to refuse those suspected of trafficking in drink a fair trial; imprisonment, hard labour and disgrace have followed conviction; yet the one result of it all has been—failure '

Iowa is a thinly populated, somewhat newly settled State, almost in the centre of the Union, with about

2,000,000 inhabitants, of whom one-sixth are foreigners, chiefly Germans. It must be remembered, in attempting to form any true estimate of the causes of the failure of the law, that Iowa suffers from the usual weaknesses of youth, whether youth of nations or of individuals,—venturesomeness and fickleness. Its people are excitable, inclined to experimentalise, and apt to rush to extremes. The spirit of respect for the law because it is law, so universal in England, is very little known there. If the law suits the people of a city or a county they will observe it; if not, then so much the worse for the law! In one town the inhabitants will be endowed with remarkable virtue : boys caught smoking will be liable to have the stick of the policeman across their backs ; the sale of cigarettes, even to adults, will be forbidden ; ballet dancers, if permitted at all, will be ordered to wear long skirts ; saloons will be unknown ; men as well as women found in houses of ill-fame will be summarily arrested and punished ; and, in short, the municipality will devise sumptuary laws about almost everything belonging to the public and private life of the people. In the next town, possibly only a few miles off, the other extreme will prevail : gambling dens and saloons, although both illegal by the laws of the State, will be allowed to carry on their business unmolested by the police, on the payment of regular monthly fines ; there will be a quarter of legalised ill-fame, as in any Japanese city, and public women will be inspected and certificated as in Paris. The people of Iowa have not yet definitely made up their minds whether they shall make their State (by order of the Legislature and with the approval of the Governor) into a Paradise on earth, or whether they shall permit one another to go to the bad, and shall make the road that way as smooth as possible. Meanwhile they are experimenting both ways; and in course of time, when the disorderly elements have been controlled, and the effervescent stage of State life is passed, Iowa will probably settle down to a great and glorious future.

The prohibitory law here, as enacted in 1884 and revised in the following years, bears in its general regulations forbidding the sale of intoxicants as a beverage a family resemblance to those of Maine and Kansas already described. Necessary sales for medicinal purposes are made through duly licensed chemists; but a chemist is not allowed to sell to any one unless the applicant is known personally to him, or bears a letter of recommendation from some reliable person of his acquaintance. The would-be purchaser has to fill up the following form :—

"I hereby make request for the purchase of the following intoxicating liquors (quantity and kind). My true name is . . . I am not a minor, and I reside in . . . Township, in the County of . . . State of . . . The actual purpose for which this request is made is to obtain the liquor for (myself, wife, child, or name of the person it is intended for) for medicinal use, and neither myself nor the said (wife, child, etc.) habitually uses intoxicating liquors as a beverage."

If the applicant is not known to the chemist, the following form has to be filled in by some other person :—

"I hereby certify that I am acquainted with . . . the applicant for the purchase of the foregoing described liquors, and that said . . . is not a minor, and is not in the habit of using intoxicating liquors as beverage, and is worthy of credit as to the truthfulness of statements in the foregoing request, and my residence is . . ."

At the end of each two months the chemist has to send in to the county auditor all application forms received by him, with a sworn statement attached, "that no liquors have been sold or dispensed under colour of my permit during said months, except as shown by the requests herewith returned, and that I have faithfully complied with the conditions of my oath".

The penalties for selling liquor without a permit, or for keeping for the purpose of unlawful sale, are, for the first offence, 50 dollars to 100 dollars fine ; for subsequent convictions, 300 dollars to 500 dollars fine, and imprisonment for not more than six months. But there is a more severe method of proceeding against offenders. An injunction may be obtained for the closing of any premises where liquors are unlawfully sold, on the plea of their being a nuisance. If they are again opened after this, the offender is liable to a fine of up to 1000 dollars, and imprisonment for six months or a year. Courts and juries are required to so construe the law as to prevent any evasion, and even the general repute of a house may be brought as evidence against it. When the injunction method is used, there is no trial by jury, and thus a conviction can be secured in localities where public opinion is most opposed to the law.

Police officers are bound to inform on offenders, under pain of loss of office and heavy fines. Drunken persons are liable to a month's imprisonment, unless they give information as to who supplied them with liquor; any one who buys liquor unlawfully can compel the seller to return him the money paid for it; and when a person gets drunk the seller can not only be compelled to pay all costs incurred by any one in attending to his customer, but is also liable to an action for civil damages from any relative or connection of the drunken man who is injured in person, property or means of support by such intoxication. It will be noticed that the law directs its penalties against the seller rather than the purchaser.

The Act was carried by a Republican majority, and has been fiercely opposed by the Democrats. At first the new provisions were observed in about eighty-five out of ninety-nine counties in the State, the parts refusing obedience being mostly those along the banks of the Mississippi and most thickly populated. In these latter it was found impossible, in spite of the strictest provisions, to secure even an outward show of observance. Rum-sellers, police, justices, and the newspapers all combined to ignore the law. Temperance men sought to secure convictions, but in vain. When there seemed any likelihood of a specially active reformer making trouble, the

saloon element did not hesitate to use force to put him
down.   The most notable case of this was that of Dr. G.
C. Haddock, a warm prohibitionist, who lived at Sioux
City, where the law was ignored.   He spoke and wrote,
started prosecutions, and used every means in his power
against the drink interest.   One night, as he was re-
turning home, he was surrounded in the open street by a
crowd of roughs, and one man deliberately shot him in
the face, killing him immediately.   A prominent liquor
man was arrested for the offence, and it is said that the
evidence against him was overwhelming.   Nevertheless,
the local authorities delayed bringing him to trial for as
long as possible, and then he was acquitted.   It was
openly alleged that the jury had been specially selected
to secure this result, and had been heavily bribed.

Yet, in spite of these serious drawbacks, the law at
first had some measure of success.   Governor Larrabee,
in retiring from office in 1890, referred at some length to
the results obtained from it, in his message to the Legislature.   Though his words cannot be said to be free from
prejudice, they yet must carry weight as being the official
verdict of the leading officer of the State.   "The benefits
which have resulted," he declared, "from the enforcement of this law are far-reaching indeed.   It is a well-
recognised fact that crime is on the increase in the
United States, but Iowa does not contribute to that
increase.   While the number of convicts in the country
at large rose from 1 in every 3442 of population in
1850 to 1 in every 860 in 1880, the ratio in Iowa at

present is only 1 in every 3130. The gaols of many
counties are now empty during a good portion of the
year, and the number of convicts in our penitentiaries
has been reduced from 750 in March, 1886, to 604 on
1st July, 1889. It is the testimony of the judges of our
courts that criminal business has been reduced from
30 to 75 per cent., and that criminal expenses have
diminished in like proportion.

" There is a remarkable decrease in the business and
fees of sheriffs and criminal lawyers, as well as in the
number of requisitions and extradition warrants issued.
We have less paupers and less tramps in the State in
proportion to our population than ever before. Breweries
have been converted into oatmeal mills and canning
factories, and are operated as such by their owners. . . .
The poorer classes have better fare, better clothing,
better schooling, and better houses. . . . It is safe to say
that not one-tenth, and probably not one-twentieth, as
much liquor is consumed in the State now as was five
years ago."

But even while Governor Larrabee wrote these words
the knell of the new movement had been already
sounded, and from 1890 the cause he advocated has
been steadily losing ground in the State. His successor,
Governor Boies, was notoriously opposed to prohibition,
and threw the whole weight of his authority against
efficient enforcement. He declared the suppression of
the drink traffic to be an impossibility, and that to
attempt it is " a cruel violation of one of the most valued

of human rights". As though to make his own asser-
tions come true, he pardoned by the wholesale persons
convicted of unlawful selling. The result was what
might be expected. In all communities where the
authorities had been not over-warm about enforcement
they now became slack, and everywhere the police
said that it was useless to secure convictions merely for
the Governor to make out pardons. In more than one
town and county where the trade had long been kept
under, it now again made its appearance, and soon the
last state of Iowa was worse than the first. Most of the
teetotalers seemed to lose heart and do nothing; while
for the few who were active the dynamiter's bomb, the
incendiary's torch and the murderer's revolver were ready
to silence them into submission.

But all the blame must not be laid on Governor Boies.
He could not have assumed the attitude he did had he
not been supported by a large proportion of the people.
His conduct was approved by the State in general, as may
be seen by the fact that in 1891 he was re-elected for the
Governorship by a majority twice as large as that he had
previously secured. Iowa had tired of its anti-liquor
crusade.

The condition of affairs in many parts in 1893 was a
disgrace to the whole State. At Council Bluffs, a town
of slightly over 20,000 inhabitants, no attempt was made to
secure enforcement, and about seventy saloons were wide
open. The city had made regulations of its own to deal
with this and similar evils. Drink shops were allowed to

do business undisturbed on paying the City Treasury 52 dollars 10 cents a month ; gambling hells were required to pay 100 dollars a month ; houses of ill-fame 12 dollars 10 cents a month, and the inmates of such places 8 dollars 10 cents each.

In Carroll, a town of 3000 inhabitants, a similar plan was adopted, and seventeen saloons and four wholesale dealers were allowed to go free on paying 20 dollars each monthly, as a town licence.   In the whole of Carroll county the law was ignored.   At Des Moines, with a population of 50,000, the amount of drunkenness had been rapidly increasing ever since Boies took office.   In 1890, out of 2441 total arrests, 940 were for drunkenness ; in 1891, out of 2921 the number of drink cases was 1015 ; in 1892, 1113 out of a total of 3345 were for drunkenness.   In Davenport, with 3000 inhabitants, largely Germans, there were beer gardens and saloons running open week days and Sundays, as free from concealment as though they were in the Fatherland.   The houses of ill-fame have been licensed here, confined to a certain quarter of the city, and their inmates inspected weekly and given certificates of health.   The keepers of such houses are made to pay monthly fees of 25 dollars, and the inmates 10 dollars.   A fee of 200 dollars a year was required from saloon keepers, and those who refused to pay were subjected to all manner of annoyances from the municipality.[1]

[1] For many of these particulars about the condition of affairs in Iowa in 1893 I am indebted to the *Toronto Globe* for November

It would be wearisome to go on further.   Hardly a
town in the State, besides many country parts, but had
abandoned prohibition, not for licence and control, but
for a lawless free trade, tempered by the levying of municipal blackmail.

It was manifest that this condition of affairs could not
last; and the Republican party, that had for many years
remained steadfast to the cause, at last determined to
abandon it.   A purposely vague clause was chosen for
the party platform in 1893, stating that "prohibition is
no test of Republicanism.   The General Assembly has
given to the State a prohibitory law as strong as any that
has ever been enacted by any country.   Like any other
criminal statute, its retention, modification, or repeal
must be determined by the General Assembly, elected
by and in sympathy with the people ; and to them is
relegated the subject to take such action as they may
deem just and best in the matter, maintaining the law in
those portions of the State where it is now or can be
made efficient, and giving the localities such methods of

and December, 1893. This journal, with enterprise that is deserv-
ing of all commendation, sent two representatives, one an avowed
prohibitionist and the other opposed to prohibition, to Iowa and
Kansas, in order to gather full particulars of the results obtained
from the liquor laws there.   The two commissioners, Messrs. J.
E. Atkinson and J. A. Ewan, performed their mission excellently,
and their reports are of more than temporary value.   I may, however, add that I have by no means solely depended on the reports
of these gentlemen in ascertaining the condition of Iowa.   Other
accounts, from varied sources, all tend to show the disgraceful and
deplorable condition of this State under the law that failed.

controlling and regulating the liquor traffic as will best serve the cause of temperance and morality."

It was fully understood at this election that the Republicans would now advocate some modification of the law, and on this understanding their candidate for Governorship was returned to office by a large majority. The newly elected Governor, the Hon. F. D. Jackson, dealt with the question at some length in his inaugural address. "A trial of ten years has demonstrated," he said, "that in many counties it (prohibition) has fully met the expectation of its friends, having successfully driven the saloon system out of existence in those counties. While this is true, there are other localities where open saloons have existed during this period of time in spite of the law, and in spite of the most determined efforts to close them. In such localities the open saloon exists without restraint or control, a constant menace to the peace and safety of the public. From these localities there is an earnest demand for relief—a demand not from the law-defying saloon sympathiser, but from the best business element—from the best moral sentiment of such communities—from the churches and from the pulpit. While the present prohibitive principle, which is so satisfactory to many counties and communities of our State, should remain in force, wisdom, justice and the interests of temperance and morality demand that a modification of this law should be made applicable to those communities where the saloon exists, to the end of reducing the evils of the liquor traffic to the minimum."

A measure for the semi-legislation of saloons had been brought forward in 1893. The malcontents did not ask for the total repeal of the law, but they demanded that, in localities where prohibition had notoriously failed, some other measures should be tried. At the end of March, 1894, a "mulct-tax" Bill was carried in the House of Representatives, and sent on at once to the Senate, where it was "railroaded" through without debate. Early in April it received the sanction of the Governor and became law. This measure is not a licensing law, and does not (nominally) license the saloon; but it provides that, on the payment by a saloon-keeper of a special tax, and on the observance of certain conditions, he shall not be liable to punishment for breaking the prohibitory law. This sounds somewhat strange to those of us who still retain old-fashioned opinions about the necessity for enforcing all laws or repealing them. Clause 16 of the "mulct" Act is surely a curiosity among illogical compromises: "Nothing in this Act contained shall in any way be construed to mean that the business of the sale of intoxicating liquors is in any way legalised, nor is the same to be construed in any manner or form as a licence, nor shall the assessment or payment of any tax for the sale of liquors as aforesaid protect the wrong-doer from any penalties now provided by law, except that on conditions hereinafter provided certain penalties may be suspended".

The tax required from liquor-sellers is 600 dollars a year, besides a bond for 3000 dollars. If, in a town of

5000 inhabitants, a majority of the electors who voted at the last poll sign a written statement consenting to the establishment of saloons; or if, in a place with less than 5000 inhabitants, sixty-five per cent. of the electors sign a similar statement, then, in such places the fact that a liquor-seller has paid his tax shall be a bar to any proceedings under the prohibitory Acts. Each saloon is to consist of a single room, with only one exit and entrance, with the bar in plain view from the street, and with no chairs or furniture except such as are necessary for the attendants. The attendants must all be males, and no liquor is to be sold to minors, drunkards, persons who have taken "drink cures," or to any person "whose wife, husband, parent, child, brother, sister, guardian, ward over fourteen years of age, or employer shall by written notice forbid such sales ".

It is too early yet to say what the result of the "mulct" Act will be. The latest news from Iowa reports that the necessary proportion of signatures for the opening of saloons has been obtained in a number of moderate-sized towns, which were formerly thought to be favourably inclined to prohibition. In Des Moines 5500 signatures have been secured, and the drink-sellers boast that they can obtain one or two thousand more if required. It is yet a matter of doubt whether the saloon-keepers in several border towns will submit to the new law or will continue their old plan; but it seems certain, that for a large part of the State the days of even nominal prohibition are over. The State Legisla-

ture has agreed to re-submit to popular vote the prohibitory amendment to the Constitution; but this is
done rather as a sop to the advocates of temperance
than with the expectation that it will lead to any
change.

CHAPTER VI.

HIGH LICENCE.

HIGH licence in its present form is comparatively a new development of American drink legislation. During the early part of the latter half of this century reformers would hear of nothing but the most uncompromising prohibition. Then came a reaction, and even the stoutest opponents of the liquor traffic were forced to admit that in towns of any size prohibition has never yet been a success. As a leading reformer put it: "Prohibition has not yet touched the question where it presents the gravest difficulties, except to fail. After an existence of more than fifty years it has yet to grapple with this problem in any great centre of population. A law unenforced in its essential particulars debauches the public conscience." The question at last had to be faced—how, as men will have drink, the traffic in it can be conducted so as to do the least harm to the community. This led to high licence, a policy which includes the limiting the number of saloons, placing them under strict regulations, and fixing the licence fee at such a high rate as will keep all but responsible men out of the business. This plan would, it was hoped, meet the legitimate demand for drink, exterminate low saloons,

and at the same time bring in a very considerable revenue, thus applying Emerson's maxim, and "making the
backs of our vices bear the burden of our taxes".

As a general rule the high licence movement has been
supported by the Church and the Roman Catholic
temperance societies, but has received bitter opposition
from more extreme abstainers. "High licence is a fraud
and a failure," said Neal Dow not long since; "and the
greatest hindrance to the temperance movement in
America is the Church Temperance Society, which
supports it." Liquor-sellers look on it with mingled
feelings. Where there is a likelihood of prohibition
becoming law they openly support high licence. Thus the
Maine Hotel Keepers' Association recently passed a
resolution that "local option and high licence is the
best means of dealing with the liquor question". But,
where temperance sentiment is weak, the saloon-keepers
not unnaturally do their best to maintain the old lax
low-licence regulations.

The new method first came to the front at Nebraska
in 1881, by the passing there of the "Slocumb law,"
which fixed the State licensing fees at 500 dollars for
saloons in small towns, and double that amount where
the population exceeded 10,000. From Nebraska the
idea spread rapidly, and was soon adopted by many other
States. The most conspicuous instance of its working is
to be found in Pennsylvania, where the Brooks Licensing
Act passed through the Legislature in 1887, and came
into force on 1st June, 1888. The leading provisions of

the Brooks Act are, that the granting of licences shall be
left in the hands of the Courts of Quarter Sessions, which
shall issue whatever number they deem necessary, with
full power to revoke any or all at the end of each twelve
months; that each licensee shall pay a fee of from 1000
dollars downwards, according to the size of the town or
city in which he carries on his trade ; and, furthermore,
besides his giving a personal bond for 2000 dollars, two
owners of real estate living in the immediate neighbourhood shall also become bondsmen to the same amount
each, as sureties for his strictly keeping the law. To
these clauses are added the prohibitions, usual in most of
the States, against selling on Sundays or election days,
or to minors or intoxicated persons. As an immediate
result of the passing of the Act, the number of licensed
houses in Philadelphia was reduced from 6000 to about
1300, and in other parts of the State even greater reductions. were made. The judges used their discretionary
powers to a considerable extent, and for every successful
applicant for a licence there were two others willing to
find sureties and to pay the fees, but whose applications
were refused. Yet, notwithstanding the reduced number
of saloons, the revenue showed a most decided increase.
Before the passing of the Act the licensing fees in Philadelphia came to 300,000 dollars ; now, with less than a
quarter of the former number of houses, they amounted to
680,000 dollars, and the whole State derived an annual
drink revenue of close on 2,000,000 dollars. It is worth
noting in this connection that the total amount of criminal

and charitable expenses in Philadelphia alone caused
through excessive drinking comes to over 2,000,000 dollars
annually.

The law had an immediate and most remarkable effect
on crime. The number of committals to Philadelphia
county prison for the twelve months before the passing
of the Act was 27,867 ; for the twelve months afterwards
it was only 18,218. The number of Sunday arrests and
committals for intoxication during the same two periods
was—before, 1263; after, 381 ; showing a reduction of
about 70 per cent. The number of women arrested sank
to less than one-third, from 138 to 41.

These good results cannot, however, be solely attributed
to the fact that the licence fees are heavy. "The real
virtue of an Act such as we have in this State," said a
local journal in 1890, "lies not in the high fee, but in the
restrictions put upon the issuance of licences. . . . The
fee is the least important feature of the Brooks Act." In
Philadelphia there is a strong public opinion to back up
the Act; and the police are, on the whole, active in
searching for evasions. The great obstacles in the way
of the total suppression of unlicensed houses lie in the
two facts that juries are not always willing to convict, and
that the courts have a way of letting the cases run on for
an unconscionable time, until it is almost impossible to
bring witnesses to secure proof of the offences. For
instance, it was reported by the Police Department in
November, 1891, that since June in that year there had
been 325 arrests for unlawful sale, etc. ; 242 of these

were returned to court; in 204 cases were true bills
found, only 99 cases had been fully tried (out of which
76 convictions were secured), and there were no less
than 103 cases awaiting trial, and 28 more awaiting the
action of the grand jury.

Since the first year, the licensing judges in Philadelphia
have gone in for increasing the number of saloons, and
proportionately with the increase of liquor shops the total
of arrests for intoxication has risen.   There were 32,974
persons taken up by the police for intoxication and disorderly conduct the year before the passing of the Act,
while for the year afterwards there were only 19,887.
For the twelve months from June 1, 1890, the number
of saloons was increased to about 2000, and the committals at once rose to over 25,000.

In the next licensing year the number of houses was
again reduced, and once more the number of arrests
showed a reduction, though not proportionately large.
Last year the judges decided to increase the number;
and it is to be feared that if they do not stop this course
the amount of drunkenness will soon be as great as it was
before the passing of the Act.   Thoughtful citizens are
widely awake to the evils of this course, and great
pressure has been brought to bear on the judges to
abandon their present policy.   In September, 1893, the
local Law and Order League sent a letter round to many
of the leading inhabitants on this matter; and through
the courtesy of its secretary I am able to reproduce parts
of it here.   "Persistent efforts have been and are still

being made," the Committee stated, "to induce the
court to increase the number of liquor licences. . . . We
have reason to believe that a large number of applications
have been and will be made in the interests of a few individuals who manage to evade the law, which does not
allow an applicant to be interested in more than one
licensed place—thus you will see that the greatest vigilance has to be exercised in dealing with this subject.

"There were 224 more licences granted from 1st June,
1893, than for the previous year; and the number of
arrests for intoxication in the last three months, ending
1st September, as compared with the same period of
time in the previous year, shows the following result :—

Year.		No. of licences.	No. of arrests.
1892	June to September	1928	7056
1893	,,	,,	2181	7375

—an increase of 319 over the previous year."

In some cities, the Brooks law has, for a time at least,
apparently led to an increase of the very evils it was
framed to check.   Thus, in Pittsburg the number of
saloons was cut down from 1500 to 244, and finally
to less than 100, yet the arrests for intoxication went up
by 10 per cent.

But further investigation shows that this result has
been brought about by the open, unchecked setting the
Act at defiance. "Speak-easies" (that is, unlicensed
saloons) have been allowed to spring up in such numbers
that five years ago there were probably seven to each
licensed house. These places were permitted to exist

because of the political power of their owners, and the
police did not dare proceed against them. The agent
of the local Law and Order League opened prosecutions
against about 150 such houses in a couple of years; but
in nearly every instance the juries refused to convict.
It has been openly stated time after time that both the
police and juries are under the control of the liquor
ring, though just now there is admittedly a great improvement in this respect. At ordinary times the
"speak-easies" are conducted with at least a show of
secrecy, getting their liquor in at night, and thinly dis-
guising themselves as cigar shops, drug stores, or eating
houses; but during elections they sometimes throw off
even the appearance of concealment, knowing that no one
will venture to attack them. At the election of January,
1890, the local *Commercial Gazette* reported: "On Sunday
not a few of the select seven hundred were running wide
open. They were not 'speak-easies,' but 'yell-louds,' as
they disturbed their neighbourhoods with their hideous
conduct. What inducements have regularly-licensed
saloons to observe the law and renew their licences in
the spring if saloons that pay no licence are permitted
to sell not only throughout the week but on Sundays,
when of all days they should be kept shut? The 'speak-
easies' have, or imagine they have, a 'pull' on the
political parties, that they thus dare to impudently
disregard the law." A partial failure of the Act has
been caused in other places besides Pittsburg by the
presence of such houses; and even where the police do

their utmost it is no easy matter to exterminate them. The Chief of Police in Lancaster county reported in 1889 that there was a considerable amount of drunkenness among women and young people; and that the drink was obtained, not in licensed houses, "but in hell-holes known as beer-clubs, or in houses where beer is delivered in quantities". From other parts come similar reports.

Unquestionably, high licence, when properly enforced, is a check to intemperance; with an unbiassed executive, an uncorrupted police and a law-abiding community, it does much to rob the liquor traffic of many of its evils. But, unfortunately, these conditions are not to be found in many American cities. All who have studied the working of the law admit that the mere fact that a licence fee is high is not enough in itself; this must go along, as it does in most places, with a large measure of local control and with wise restrictive legislation. The great fault of the high-licence plan is that it leaves the saloon almost as great a power in politics as ever. But how this is to be prevented, short of sweeping the drink-sellers away altogether, does not appear.

PART II.

GREATER BRITAIN.

CHAPTER I.

PROHIBITION AND LOCAL OPTION IN CANADA.

WHILE Great Britain has been content, for many years, to do little more than talk about proposed temperance legislation, Greater Britain has been active in framing laws, testing them by actual practice, and revising, strengthening or abandoning them as the results have shown to be advisable. Our colonial cousins, free from the prejudices and cast-iron traditions of English political life, have displayed far more willingness to adopt strong remedies for a grave disease than have we ourselves at home. In Canada the drink question has been, for over a quarter of a century, one of the most pressing problems in Dominion politics; and the results of efforts made to solve it there should prove of real value to law-makers on both sides of the Atlantic. Compared with England, Canada is decidedly a sober country. In some parts total abstinence is the rule rather than the exception; the average consumption of liquor is comparatively small;

and the liquor traffic has been for years under strict
regulation. Though the licensing laws differ in the
various provinces, they are everywhere much in advance
of our own. Sunday closing is universal, no drink can
be sold on election days, and in most districts the taverns
have to be shut up on Saturdays at six or seven in the
evening. High licence prevails in many of the cities,
the penalties for serving minors or drunken persons are
very heavy, and a limited form of local option gives
communities power to sweep away almost all of the
drink shops in their borders. The result of these
measures may be seen in the fact that while in England
the annual consumption of drink is thirty-four gallons
per head, in Canada it is only four.

Early in the seventies, the temperance party started
an agitation to obtain out-and-out prohibition. Petitions
poured in on Parliament, and such pressure was brought
to bear on individual members that the Dominion
Government finally decided to introduce an Act which
would give the people in every city and county the right
to interdict the traffic there. The framing of the measure
was left in the hands of the Hon. Robert Scott, a well-
known lawyer and a member of the Government, and he
drew up a Bill which seemed at the time as stringent
and as workable as possible. The "Scott Act," as it
was at once universally called, provided that on one-
quarter of the electors of any city or town petitioning the
Governor-General, he should cause a direct vote to be
taken as to whether the place was to come under the

Act or not. A bare majority would decide either way;
and once the election was held, the question could not
be re-opened for three years. At the end of three years,
the defeated party might demand another poll. If the
people decided to come under the Act, all licences in
their district would lapse at the end of the year, without
any compensation being paid to the licence holders, and
then the ordinary manufacture or sale of intoxicating
liquors as a beverage would be absolutely prohibited.
The penalties provided for attempting to evade the law
were—50 dollars for the first offence, 100 dollars for the
second, and not more than two months' imprisonment
for each subsequent conviction. Everything was done
to make the recovery of the penalties as simple as
possible; there was no power of appeal, and, while it
was the special duty of the collectors of Inland Revenue
to see that the law was enforced, any private individual
had the power to institute a prosecution.

The Scott Act was received with almost universal
approbation; Macdonald and Mackenzie, the two leading
Canadian statesmen, supported it; and in May, 1878, it
was read for a second time in the Dominion House of
Commons without a division. It received the Royal
Assent the same month, and became law. Within the
next seven years it was submitted to seventy-seven
electoral districts, and was accepted by sixty-one. The
majorities for it were usually overwhelmingly large. In
York, 1215 electors voted for the Act, and only 69
against; in Prince the figures stood, 2062 for, 271

against; and in many other places the proportion was about the same. But the hot enthusiasm for prohibition did not last very long. Communities that had voted to go under the Act became first lukewarm and then hostile; and soon a repeal movement set in, almost as strong as the demand for prohibition that had preceded it. The revenue returns showed, it is true, a most decided diminution in the consumption of liquor. Comparing the statistics for the ten years ending 1888 with those for the ten ending in 1878, the *per capita* reduction was 39 per cent. in spirits, 8 per cent. in beer, and 49 per cent. in wine. But this apparent reduction was almost altogether neutralised by the great increase in smuggling. The coast line of the seaboard provinces is so extensive that even the utmost vigilance of the revenue authorities cannot altogether put this down. The extent to which it prevailed may be shown by the estimate of Lieutenant-Colonel Forsythe, chief of the police at Quebec, that in a single year 5000 barrels of liquor were landed by smugglers at one place, St. Pierre Miquelon.[1]

What was the cause of this change of sentiment? Perhaps the principal reason was an unfortunate dispute which arose between the Dominion and the provincial authorities as to whether the right to pass laws dealing

---

[1] This statement was made before the Royal Commission on the Liquor Traffic. At the time of writing this, the official reports of the evidence given before the Commission are not yet issued; consequently, I am obliged to rely on the somewhat abridged accounts given in the Canadian daily papers.

with the drink traffic lay with the former or the latter. The provincial authorities declared that the Central Parliament was exceeding its powers in passing such a measure, and the point was fought out before the courts. After various decisions by the lower courts, the Judicial Committee of the Privy Council declared, in June, 1882, that the Scott Act was constitutional. Then the provincial and local authorities practically refused to take steps to ensure the active enforcement of the Act. They said that as it was a Dominion, and not a provincial measure, the Dominion Parliament must see to it. Political issues became mixed up with the question of enforcement, and in many parts law-breakers well understood that the local authorities would take no active steps to bring them to justice, if they could avoid doing so.

Senator Scott, the framer of the law, himself admits that this is the true explanation. In a recent interview he said : " The provisions for enforcing the law were full and complete. But there is no Act in the statute books that was more bitterly opposed ; some of the judges in the maritime provinces even refused to give effect to it. The law was fought out in every court in the land; and until the Judicial Committee of the Privy Council sustained it, the attempt at enforcement was hopeless. Neither Governments nor courts regarded it with favour. The onus of enforcing the law was cast upon the Federal Government, yet that Government could not be charged with showing any disposition to enforce the law. . . .

The temperance element in very many localities either condemned the omission of the executive to put the law into operation, or became indifferent on the subject. Wherever there was a strong temperance sentiment, as in many counties in the maritime provinces, the law was enforced by the people, and it has borne good fruit." [1]

The case of Ontario, which has excited special interest in England, may be taken as in many respects a typical one. The temperance party is very strong here, and the Act was adopted in 1884 and 1885 by about two-thirds of the province. A vigorous attempt was made to enforce it, and at first with some show of success. The consumption of liquor was for a time diminished, the saloons put up their shutters or sold only temperance drinks, and illegal traders were quickly brought to book. Mr. W. J. Thomas, a Toronto brewer, has given the following as the experience of his firm with the Scott Act: "I found my output to decrease during the Scott Act years, and to change in character. It was sneaked into Scott Act towns by night, and in all sorts of boxes, barrels, and other packages. There was also a large increase in the bottle trade, as well as more bought for private families."

But soon trouble came. Legal authorities raised difficulties in the way of maintaining the law, and convictions were often quashed on appeal on the slightest

[1] *Montreal Daily Star*, 29th December, 1893.

grounds. The pro-liquor party showed fight, and persons who attempted to give evidence against drink-sellers would have their windows broken, would suffer personal violence, and would be publicly denounced as "sneaks" and "spies". A system of intimidation was organised, magistrates who convicted were openly insulted and threatened, notable temperance workers had their houses blown up or their ricks fired, and informers went in danger of their lives. After a time, moreover, the commitments for drunkenness showed a considerable increase; in 1876, they were 3868; in 1887, when the Act was in force, they had mounted to 4130; and in 1892, after the repeal of the Act, they were only 2736. This increase of drunkenness under prohibition was probably due to the fact that people became addicted to whisky, owing to its being portable, rather than beer, which they could not so easily smuggle or hide.

The story of a publican, given before the Royal Commission, is of interest, as showing how drink-sellers evaded the law. "I had two years' experience of the Scott Act at Port Huron, a town of 2000 inhabitants," said Mr. J. C. Miller. "I complied with the Scott Act at my hotel there for three months, but the receipts would not justify perpetuity. On the 12th July I made a drink called 'conundrum drink,' composed of water, lemons and whisky. This was supplemented by lager, called for the day 'blue ribbon beer'. The temperance men sent up two detectives from Kincardine, who were low characters, and would swear to anything. When they came to give

6

evidence, I gave them forty dollars to clear me, and they did so.

"Dr. McLeod (a Commissioner).—You paid them the money to perjure themselves ?

"Mr. Miller.—Well, I gave them forty dollars, and do not know whether they got liquor in my place or not. They were prepared to swear that they did, and they swore that they didn't. I then tried the experiment of keeping the liquor to give away, and it was entirely successful. Then I sold cider, and gave the liquor away. That was also successful ; and after the temperance men sought several times to secure a conviction without success, they let me alone, and I sold freely until the Act was repealed."

It must not be supposed that the temperance people were passive spectators of these attempts to defy the law. On the contrary, they were active in prosecuting. The number of prosecutions for breaches of the law in the six months ending in July, 1886, was 1005 ; for the six months ending in October, 1887, the number of prosecutions was 2845. The number of convictions in the first period was 541, and in the second period 1771.

The electors of Ontario had enough of the law, and at the earliest possible opportunity the Act was repealed in every county in the province.

Mr. F. S. Spence, the secretary of the Dominion Alliance, gave the following as the reasons why (in the opinion of prohibitionists) the law was repealed :—

"(1) Because the people were disappointed in finding that it did not give them a fuller measure of prohibition.

"(2) Because of the hard feeling engendered among neighbours by the forcing of evidence.

"(3) Because of the annoyance caused by the hotel-keepers closing their houses, and of the terrorism practised.

"(4) Because of the inefficiency of the machinery for the enforcing of the Act.

"(5) Because the vote for repeal was often brought on prematurely during a time of local irritation over the effects of the Act.

"(6) Because of antagonistic personal influence."

The temperance party did not take its defeat quietly. It maintained that the failure was due, not to any mistake in the principle of prohibition, but to erroneous legislation and weakness of administration ; and a fresh agitation was soon started for a more perfect measure. But for some time action was delayed. The great stumbling-block in the way of the authorities doing anything is the doubt whether the right to legislate lies with the federal or the provincial authorities. The decision of the Privy Council in 1882, while settling the legality of the Scott Act, by no means made clear the exact line of demarcation between the powers of the greater and lesser Legislatures on this matter. In order to settle this, the Ontario Government has submitted to the Supreme Court a constitutional case which will clear up the matter. As soon as this is decided there, it will be taken on to the

Privy Council, and it is expected that by early next year the matter may be finally settled.

This doubt has given Dominion politicians a very good excuse for doing nothing. " When we get a prohibition law in Ontario," said Sir Oliver Mowatt, the Ontario Premier, in answer to a deputation (20th April, 1893), " we will want one that is enforced. There is no use in a nominal prohibition, no use in putting a prohibition law on the statute book, unless we can, and do, enforce it. You all know that a prohibition law is difficult of enforcement, as there are too many people interested in its not being enforced. If a law is not enforced to any extent, it is a thousand times worse than if there was no such law on the statute book. Any prohibition law under the present condition of public sentiment is difficult of enforcement; and if there were any reasonable doubt as to whether that law is valid or not, it would be hopeless to attempt to enforce it. We may be sorry for that, and unwilling to believe it; but if we endeavour to enforce in this country a prohibition law, when there is not a reasonable certainty of its being valid, it will be a hopeless task."

Year by year, since their defeats in 1887 and 1888, the prohibitionists have been gaining greater political power, and they now command so many votes that neither party can afford to ignore them. In order to make a show of satisfying their demand, and at the same time, perhaps, to shelve the question for a year or two, the Dominion Government appointed, in 1892, a Royal

Commission to inquire into the whole subject. Since then the Commissioners have been moving from place to place, collecting a considerable amount of useful, and a still larger quantity of irrelevant and next to valueless information. The Commission has given a great many no doubt worthy persons the opportunity of airing in public their individual opinions on the folly or wisdom of total abstinence, on the exact number of ounces of alcohol it is wise to consume in a day, and on other equally absorbing themes. But if the Commissioners print *verbatim* all the evidence that has been tendered before them, their report will almost rival in bulk the holy books of the Buddhists, or the report of the Sweating Commission.

In 1893 and 1894, in order to accurately ascertain the real opinion of the people on the liquor question, the greater number of the Provincial Governments took plébiscites on prohibition. The plan was adopted from the well-known Swiss referendum; but with the great difference that, whereas in Switzerland a sufficient majority obtained by the direct vote alters the law, the plébiscites in Canada have no legislative effect whatever, but are purely expressions of opinion, taken as test of the popular will. At first the extreme left wing of the temperance party looked with some disfavour on them, and declared that they were nothing but pretexts to delay legislation.

A plébiscite was first taken in Manitoba, on the same day as the general election, at the end of 1892. Two-thirds of this province are said to be already under prohibition, by means of local option laws, and out of the forty members of the Legislature twenty-two are reputed total abstainers. The vote was taken on the single question : " Do you think the prohibition of the manufacture and sale of intoxicating liquor desirable? Yes or No." The number of votes recorded was fairly large, being only a little over five per cent. less than that cast for the candidates for the Legislature. The result was a complete victory for the prohibitionists. Even Winnipeg, the largest city, which was reckoned a very doubtful place, gave a majority of 1300 for prohibition. The result in the whole province was:—

Total votes for candidates,	...	...	...	28,204
Total votes on prohibition,	...	...	...	26,752
For prohibition, ...	...	...	...	19,637
Against prohibition,	...	...	...	7,115
Majority for prohibition, ...	...	...	...	12,522

The Provincial Assembly has since requested the Dominion Parliament to give effect to the popular vote by legislative enactment.

In Prince Edward Island a plébiscite has shown a majority of 7000 in favour of prohibition ; and in Nova Scotia, where a poll has just been taken, the result has been a majority of 31,701 for prohibition. But the most surprising result of all has come from Ontario. It was generally anticipated by those not on the spot that this province, with its former unfortunate experience, would hardly again support a proposal for the suppression of the drink traffic. A vote was taken on New Year's Day,

1894; and all persons having votes at municipal elections, and all unmarried women and widows who exercise the franchise, were allowed to take part. No elector had more than one vote. The question submitted was : " Are you in favour of the immediate prohibition by law of the importation, manufacture and sale of intoxicating liquors as a beverage ? "

The temperance party made great preparations for the election. Innumerable meetings were held, committees of ladies canvassed the voters, ministers urged on their congregations the duty of rightly using their electoral powers, and all that was possible to ensure success was done. The teetotalers in Ontario undoubtedly anticipated a victory, but even the most sanguine among them had hardly dared to anticipate such a majority as was obtained. 192,487 voted for prohibition, 110,757 against, leaving a majority in favour of 81,730 votes.

The most discouraging thing about the plébiscite is the fact that only about 58 per cent. of the electors in the province took the trouble to record their votes. The women constituted 35 per cent. of the total electors, and while the ballot forms for the men were printed on yellow paper, those for women were on blue, in order that it might be ascertained how they voted. It was found that the women were six to one for prohibition. So if the votes of the women had been taken away, the majority in favour would have been reduced to a few thousands.

But after allowing for these things, the victory was

unquestionably a notable one. The chief strength of the liquor party lay, as usual, among the foreign portion of the community, and those towns in which the Germans predominated declared by large majorities against prohibition. In Toronto the prohibitionists obtained a majority, but so many electors abstained from voting as to make this apparent victory little better than a defeat. But many places that had been confidently expected to declare for licence decided the other way. Even several districts that a few years ago almost unanimously repealed the Scott Act, had come round again in favour of prohibition.

The temperance party in Ontario is now somewhat divided. There is a noisy, if not very influential section, that is in favour of the Provincial Legislature at once passing a provincial prohibitory law, taking for granted that the Privy Council will decide in favour of the State right to do so. Happily, this section is in a minority, for no course could be more harmful to the temperance cause. If a provincial prohibitory law were passed now, magistrates would fear to enforce it fully until they knew whether it was really legal or not; cases of conviction would be the subject of unceasing appeals from court to court ; and every cause that made the Scott Act a failure would, in an accentuated degree, prevent the efficient carrying out of the new law.

Many members of the temperance party recognise this, and have determined to work for prohibition under the local option laws, and for the creation of a still stronger public sentiment against drinking, until the decision of the courts is known. Then, if it is found that the province has the right to prohibit, a Prohibition Bill will be introduced.

The Government has adopted this latter plan, and the Premier, Sir Oliver Mowatt, has given the following pledge for himself and his colleagues : " If the decision of the Privy Council should be that the province has the jurisdiction to pass a prohibitory liquor law as to sale, I will introduce such a Bill in the following Session, if I am then at the head of the Government. If the decision of the Privy Council is that the province has jurisdiction only to pass a partial prohibitory liquor law, I will introduce such a prohibitory Bill as the decision will warrant, unless the partial prohibitory power is so limited as to be ineffective from a temperance standpoint."

Prohibitionists in Ontario will only do themselves harm if they imagine that the battle for the suppression of the liquor traffic there is already won, or will be won on the passing of a suitable Act. On the contrary, it is certain that any prohibitory Bill, when passed, will meet with the greatest opposition from a considerable portion of the community. Innumerable efforts will be put forth to make it a dead letter, or to break it down in any way whatever. There is a large and controlling section of electors on whom the continuance of the law depends. It is now willing to give prohibition a trial, and if it is anything like a success it will maintain it.

But, if it should prove unworkable or unsuccessful, then the great body of the people will soon send it on the same road as the Scott Act.

So far as plébiscites have been taken throughout the Dominion, they have been in every province in favour of prohibition. There are three provinces in which there has been no voting, — New Brunswick, British Columbia, and Quebec. The last named is admitted to be, on account of the large proportion of settlers of French descent in its borders, the province least friendly to the suppression of the traffic; but the other two are generally regarded as strongholds of temperance. The opinion of New Brunswick may be seen by the following resolution passed by its Legislative Assembly on the 7th April, 1893: "Whereas, in the opinion of this Legislative Assembly, the enactment of a prohibitory liquor law would conduce to the general benefit of the people of the province, and meet with the approval of a majority of the electorate; and whereas legislative power in respect of the enactment of such law rests in the Parliament of Canada; therefore, resolved that this Assembly hereby expresses its desire that the Parliament of Canada shall, with all convenient speed, enact a law prohibiting the importation, manufacture, and sale of intoxicating liquors as a beverage, into or from the Dominion of Canada."

Many demands have been made that the Dominion Parliament, under the powers it was declared to possess by the Privy Council decision of 1882, shall immediately enact a Dominion prohibitory law. This, however, it refuses to do; and Sir John Thompson, the Dominion Premier, recently stated he can do nothing this Session, owing to the tariff reductions; and he does not think it would be a proper course to announce a policy until after the report of the Royal Commission on the question has been presented.

CHAPTER II.

LOCAL CONTROL IN NEW ZEALAND.

In no British colony is the temperance sentiment stronger, or is there more likelihood of the agitation for prohibition being brought to a successful issue, than in New Zealand. Its statesmen have shown during the last few years great political venturesomeness; the parliamentary suffrage has been given to women; social, it may be said socialistic, legislation of a most pronounced character has been encouraged, and the dreams of English Radicals have turned to blossom and fruit under the Southern Cross. The danger at present seems to be, not that the changes will be too slow, but that politicians, eager to anticipate the public wishes, may adopt and carry advanced legislation for which the colony is not prepared. This danger has been greatly increased since the passing of female suffrage. Whatever merits women may have as politicians, moderation is not one of them; and in the last election they plainly showed that they intend to select for power the men of most outspoken views and extreme policy.

New Zealand is a country of to-day, and knows but little of the social difficulties that are taxing all the energies of politicians in lands with a longer history.

The rougher and poorer emigrants have mostly chosen the other Australian colonies in preference to it, and it is peopled to-day by a picked body of prosperous Englishmen and Scotchmen. As regards the consumption of liquor, it takes almost the lowest place among those lands that fly the Union Jack. The average expenditure per head comes to only a little over three pounds a year, and the amount of proof spirits consumed per head in the same time is a little over two gallons, or only about half of the quantity drunk in England. The prohibitionist party is very strong in the colony, and is led by Sir Robert Stout, the Liberal ex-Premier. The prohibitionists do not attempt just now to secure a measure forbidding the sale of liquor throughout the colony, for they regard that as at present impracticable. Their demands for the time are local option of prohibition by a simple majority, and no compensation. This latter point they have secured; and the question of pecuniary compensation to dispossessed publicans is no longer within the range of practical politics in New Zealand. In 1892 a Licensed Victuallers' Compensation Bill was brought before the House of Representatives; but it aroused such general opposition that its proposers did not venture to ask for a division on it.

The tendency of legislation has been for some years steadily in the direction of giving increased direct power of control to the people. For some time the supervision of the drink trade was left in the hands of the various Provincial Councils, but in 1873 Sir

William Fox, then Premier, carried a measure through
Parliament which granted to two-thirds of the adult
residents in any neighbourhood the right of preventing
the issue of new licences there, on notifying their desire
in that respect by signing a petition. Eight years later,
a new Act repealed this veto law, and provided a more
complicated machinery for dealing with the question.
According to this, a Licensing Board was chosen annually
by the electors in each district, and once in every three
years the ratepayers voted on the question whether any
licences should be issued in their neighbourhood. If
they decided in the negative, the Board had to abide by
their decision ; but should they wish for an increase, the
matter was then brought before the Board, though this
body was by no means obliged to grant new licences,
even when the popular vote had given it power to do so.

In many ways this Act proved a practicable, workable
measure. The Inland Revenue returns showed each year,
from the passing of the Act up to 1889, a steady diminution
in the consumption of drink, amounting altogether in the
seven years to twenty-five per cent. ; and though this reduction has not been quite maintained during subsequent
years, the trade is still considerably less than it formerly
was. The Act stopped the increase of public-houses,
though very few of the old hotels were deprived of their
licences under it. Out of 1500 licensed houses in the
colony, only twenty-five were closed under the Act during
the first seven years. Since that time the advanced temperance party showed considerably more activity in this

direction, and succeeded in obtaining a withdrawal of most of the licences in more than one district. But a doubtful legal point cropped up, as to how far Local Boards have the power to take away old licences, that prevented very much being done. In a certain licensing district the temperance party aroused itself and succeeded in electing a Board pledged to close the hotels. The Board kept its promise, and thereupon the liquor-sellers brought a case before the courts, on the grounds that the members of the Board had publicly pledged themselves as to their line of action before election, and therefore they were biassed and did not deal with the licences in a judicial manner. The court upheld the publicans and declared that the deprival of the licences was illegal. This decision, of course, practically took from the electors the greater part of their local control. Another point in which the system proved unsatisfactory was in the supervision of licensed houses. There seems to be a general opinion among moderate men that the Boards were not nearly strict enough in bringing offending licence-holders to book.

The Act of 1883 was not sufficiently drastic to satisfy the temperance party; and last year Mr. Seddon, the Liberal Premier, brought before the Legislature and carried a liquor law which he said would meet with the approval of all parties. The measure is called "An Act to give the people greater control over the granting and refusing of licences". The licensing authority is still left in the hands of locally elected bodies : though no member of any such body can be disqualified from sitting or acting because he has at any time expressed his views or given any pledge as to the liquor traffic. The whole of the colony is now divided into sixty districts, and each of these has its own Board, consisting of the resident magistrate, and eight other residents in the district. Any elector living in a district shall be qualified to become a candidate for election to the Board there, unless he is a paid colonial or local official, or is directly or indirectly pecuniarily interested in the liquor traffic. When, once in three years, the licensing committee is elected, each voter has submitted to him at the same time three alternatives: and he must scratch out two of these, thus voting for the one he leaves untouched, or his paper will be void. The three choices are :—

(1) I vote that the number of publicans' licences continue as at present.

(2) I vote that the number of publicans' licences be reduced.

(3) I vote that no publicans' licences be granted.

No vote for a committee-man will be counted unless the elector also chooses one of these things at the same time as he votes for the members of the committee.

On the result of the direct vote the committee must act. No election is valid unless at least one-half of the voters on the register take part in it. An absolute majority of the votes recorded in any district carries either of the first two propositions, for no alteration or for reduction; but the proposal for no licences at all can only be carried on a majority of three-fifths of those voting deciding in favour of it. If the votes for no licence are under three-fifths, they are added to those for reduction, and counted as part of such. Where the proposal for reduction is successful, the committee shall carry out such reduction as it may think fit, provided that it does not exceed one-quarter of the total number of public-houses. Such licences as have been endorsed for breaches of the law since the passing of the Act are first to be taken away, and then those held in respect of premises which provide little or no accommodation for travellers beyond the bar.

The temperance party is seriously dissatisfied with this measure. "This Bill, I believe," said Sir Robert Stout in the House of Representatives, "is a Bill more in favour of the liquor traffic than if I had met the Licensed Victuallers' Association, and asked them to come to some compromise. I believe the association would have given a more reasonable Bill to the temperance party than this measure. That is my opinion, and I believe I am speaking what is correct, from what I have heard." The chief objections of the local optionists are to the clauses that provide for a three-fifths majority for prohibition, and for a 50 per cent. poll before an election is valid; they also say that the licensing areas are too large, and that the Act practically gives the publicans three years' licences. At the parliamentary elections that took place since the measure was passed, the question of a bare majority sufficing to carry the proposal for no licences has been made a test one everywhere; and the teetotalers, aided by the women's vote, have carried their point in so many places that there seems every prospect of the law being altered in this respect almost immediately.

The first licensing election under the new Act took place at the end of March, 1894. A fresh and somewhat disturbing factor was introduced in it by the voting power of the newly enfranchised women. The women were (as they had been in the parliamentary elections) by an overwhelming majority in favour of either no licences or reduction, usually the former. Sometimes they allowed their zeal to slightly outrun the bounds of womanliness. Thus, at one meeting at Christchurch, called by the leading clergy for the consideration of the question, they took possession of the hall, voted down the proposals for reduction, and refused to listen to the speakers. The chairman would not allow them to put their amendment for no licence, so they would not let the meeting continue. They were as rowdy (if reports in various local papers can be trusted) as an excited meeting at a fiercely contested election in England. Finally they determined to there and then convert one of their leading opponents. "Pastor Birch," reports the *Christchurch Weekly Press*, "says that when he came out of a meeting the ladies were hatching a conspiracy against him. They intended, when he left the meeting, to surround him in the middle of the road. A compact ring of female enthusiasts was to be formed round him, and, when they had him fairly wedged in, they intended to kneel down and pray for him. The worthy pastor, it appears, declined this delicate attention, but was at a loss how to escape. Ultimately, I believe, he hit on the device of leaving the hall supported on one side by his lordship the bishop, and on the other by Father Bell. This saved him, the women found it impossible to surround Pastor Birch without including his companions, and so let him escape."

Full reports of the results have not yet reached England, but sufficient is known to make it certain that the temperance party has gained a great victory. Had it not been for the three-fifths clause, the greater part of the country would have gone under prohibition. At the time the last mail left New Zealand, the results were known in twenty-six out of the sixty licensing divisions; and the total votes there showed that 23,752 were for prohibition, 9467 for reduction, and 16,862 for no alteration. At Wellington, where the contest excited great interest, and was looked upon as a fair test for the whole colony, the results were: for prohibition 3397, for reduction 1283, for no alteration 3581. In only one place was the necessary majority obtained for no licences, and in another place the people have decided for no bottle licences. There were quite a number of districts where the prohibitionists were only a few dozen short of the required majority.

The results have amply borne out the objection to its

being necessary for 50 per cent. of the electors to vote before the election is valid. In several places the publicans gave orders for their supporters to abstain from voting, and thus prevented public opinion being tested. At Auckland the temperance people made no attempt to prohibit or reduce, for they knew that it would be hopeless to think of securing a sufficient poll by themselves. The *New Zealand Herald* (28th March, 1894) says : " We think it will be found, when the whole of the returns come to hand, that in more than half the districts the whole proceedings are void, because half the names on the roll did not vote. The law may be defeated because one party may, previous to the elections, place a crowd of names on the roll, either merely bogus names, or the names of persons whom they know will not take the trouble to go to the poll. And as the matter stands, the ballot is practically defeated in many instances. Where there are no candidates to be voted for those acting in the interest of the hotels know, when they see a man going to the polling booth, that he is going to vote either for reduction or prohibition, and they appeal to him : ' You are surely not going to give a vote against us?' "

From what seems to be a mistaken policy, the advanced temperance party refused to take any part in the choice of committee-men; consequently, while nearly every place has chosen reduction, the amount of reduction will now be decided by men elected largely by the liquor interest. It is hard to see what benefits the prohibitionists hope to obtain from this course, unless, as many aver, they want the public-houses made as disreputable as possible, so that the people will be more eager to get rid of them.

The opinion of various classes in the colony as to the outcome of the election can, perhaps, be best seen by extracts from their own journals.   The *Lyttelton Times* (anti-prohibitionist) says : "The first really genuine local option poll has shown the people to be determined upon further reducing the number of licensed houses.   The polling, which was everywhere conducted with the most perfect decorum and good feeling, has served several useful purposes.   It has demonstrated the strength, and weakness, of the prohibition party ; it has elicited a very decided expression of public opinion that the existing number of licences is in excess of public requirements ; it has shown that the people can be safely trusted with full executive and judicial powers in a manner affecting their interests ; and it has, we hope, settled the vexed licensing question for three years to come."

The (Wellington) *New Zealand Times* says : "The present interest centres in the large prohibition vote. The weight of that vote is a surprise and a warning. Few were prepared for it, but most people frankly confessed their inability to gauge the new power.   Now that this power has declared itself, few will be prepared to deny that prohibition has come appreciably nearer than a year ago any one thought it would come in this generation. . . . The decided prohibitionist leaning of the body of electors is a warning that nothing but strict regulation, worthy of the name, will serve to stem the advancing tide."

On the other hand, the *Otago Witness*, although a strongly temperance paper, is inclined to explain away the prohibitionist vote. "Numbers of temperance people, properly so called, are working with prohibitionists," it says. "They say to themselves, 'Whatever results may be obtained from this agitation of the prohibitionists, they are sure to fall so far short of their aim that by helping them we can accomplish our own'. . . . We may yet find the bulk of the people advocating prohibition, not because it will prohibit, but because it will restrict."

The *Manawatu Daily Standard* considers: "If the present state of the public mind be any criterion, the day would seem to be dawning when prohibition will come upon us; but the feelings of many would revolt against such a revolutionary procedure being entered upon at the present time".

The *Christchurch Press* says: "The polling was nowhere so heavy as we were led to suppose by a great many enthusiasts it would be. . . . A great many abstentions may be accounted for by the fact that those whose desire was for a reduction felt pretty confident that with the votes of the no licence people it would be carried, and consequently they did not take the trouble to vote. . . . The great lesson which we learn from these elections as to the feeling of the public of New Zealand on this licensing question is that a vast majority are not prepared to go to the extreme length of closing all the houses, but that a great majority do desire that there shall be a reduction of something like 25 per cent. ; and that those which remain must be made to understand that they retain their licences only on condition that their houses are well conducted in all respects—that is to say, that they only sell good liquor to sober people within legal hours."

CHAPTER III.

A YEAR or two ago Mr. David Christie Murray stirred up the wrath of the Australians by charging them, in effect, with being the most drunken people under the sun. This statement, like most other sweeping denunciations, requires to be taken with a considerable amount of reserve; but it certainly is true that our Antipodean cousins are, to judge from the evidence afforded by their revenue returns, afflicted with a chronic and incurable thirst. The average consumption of proof alcohol in several of the colonies is almost as great as in England.

The liquor laws of Australia are now in much the same condition as many are striving to make ours at home. Local option is in force over the greater part of the continent. Sunday closing is generally compulsory, and the licensed victualler is bound by many restrictions unknown to his brother here. As each colony is entirely independent of the others, their laws differ, and must be described separately. For the purposes of this volume it will be sufficient to deal with Victoria, New South Wales and Queensland, as the laws of the remaining Australian colonies present no particular features which call for comment.

Victoria.—In Victoria, in spite of the fact that the control of the liquor traffic is almost wholly in the hands of the people themselves, the annual consumption of drink costs nearly £6 per head. This, however, is a mere trifle to what it once was, for during the gold rush in the fifties the cost was nearly £30 a head yearly for every man, woman, and child in the colony. It is misleading, however, to compare the expenditure in England and Victoria, and judge the amount consumed by it; for in the Antipodes things generally are much dearer, and money is cheaper than at home. The Victorians consume about 12 per cent. more spirits, between four and five times as much wine, and not much more than half the beer, per head of population, than we do.

From the time when Victoria separated from New South Wales down to 1876, a decidedly retrograde policy was adopted; licence fees were reduced, grocers' licences introduced, and beer shops legalised. But in the last-named year the liquor laws were amended by a measure giving limited local control over the traffic; and in 1882 a further Act was passed by which the local powers were considerably increased. Under the present law one-fifth of the electorate in any district can petition the Governor in Council to hold an election to settle the number of public-houses to be permitted there, and he is then obliged to cause a popular vote to be taken on the question. Each elector states on a ballot paper how many hotels he wishes to be licensed, and the

number named by him must be the number then existing, the statutory number, or some number between.
The statutory number has been fixed at one for every
250 inhabitants up to the first thousand, and one for
every full 500 beyond. Where the number is greater
than this it can be reduced by a poll to that limit;
where it is less, it can be raised in a similar way up to
it. But in no case can the number be reduced below
or increased above the statutory limit.

In arriving at the decision of the electors, if a majority
vote for any particular number then that number is
carried. Where, however, the votes are so scattered
that no particular number commands a majority over
all the others the following plan is adopted. "Suppose
a district with 48 hotels, and 12 as the statutory number.
Suppose, further, that 600 votes be recorded, of which
250 are for 48, 200 for 12, 20 for 13, 20 for 14, 20 for
15, 20 for 16, and 21 for 17. The votes given for the
higher numbers would be added to those given for 12
until they made a majority of votes recorded. In this
case by the time the number 17 is reached, there would
be a total of 301 votes, making a majority of the 600,
and the determination would be that the hotels be
reduced to 17."[1]

Where the electors decide in favour of a reduction,
a licensing court sits and decides what houses are to
be closed. The licensing inspector has to summon all

[1] *Victorian Alliance Annual* for 1890, Melbourne.

the hotel-keepers before the court, and the court selects the houses which are worst conducted, or which provide least accommodation, as the ones to lose their licences. The houses which are thus closed are given a monetary compensation on account of the annual value of the premises being lowered : the exact amount of the compensation is fixed by two arbitrators, appointed one by the owner and another by the minister. In case these cannot agree a county court judge or police magistrate is nominated by them as umpire. The whole of the compensation money is raised from the "trade" itself, by means of increased licensing fees and penalties for breaches of the liquor law. If these amounts are not sufficient, a special tax is imposed on liquor in order to meet the deficiency.

The amounts awarded as compensation have been, in the opinion of many, absurdly high. Thus at Ballarat East, where forty hotels were closed, the compensation awarded was, to owners, £26,126 os. 9d. ; to licensees, £13,855 18s. 4d. At Ballarat West, where twenty-six hotels were closed, the compensation came to, for owners, £12,280 ; for licensees, £8973. At Broadford the total cost of closing four places was £1220. The fact that compensation is paid makes many voters far less keen than they otherwise would be for reduction, even though the money so paid does not in any way cost them anything.

In many parts considerable use has been made of the powers of reduction. Thus in fourteen local option polls that took place in twelve months the people decided either for reduction or against increase, according as the purpose for which the poll was taken. The Victorian licensing laws have certainly prevented any considerable increase of hotels, though they have had but little effect in reducing the drink traffic itself.

The following communication from Mr. John Vale, secretary of the Victorian Alliance, shows how temperance men regard the present law. "The local option law of the colony," he writes, "first came into force in 1886; some polls were then taken, but for the most part were rendered void by the condition that one-third of the electors must record their votes in order to constitute a poll. The publican party adopted the policy of not voting, and letting it be known that all who were seen entering the polling booth would be marked men, to be injured in every possible way. Thus, the secrecy of the ballot was destroyed. Only the temperance stalwarts faced the ordeal, and we were generally just a few short of the required number. In 1887 this condition was repealed, in so far as it related to the reduction of hotels. In the following year other polls were taken with success; but then, with brewery money, a process was begun known as 'stonewalling' in the law courts. The publicans would appeal on some technical point. Being defeated on that they raised another point; and so on, until after a time they hit upon one which had something in it, or the Government got tired of the process. As a result most of the victories of 1888 were made of non-effect. We then secured a provision doing away with the power of appeal in connection with local option polls. Since then, victories have been secured in a number of important centres, and the condemned hotels have been or are now being closed. The Victorian Alliance, however, has come to the determination to promote no more polls under the present law. It is believed that polls for prohibition could be carried with no more effort than is required to win victories for reduction. The antagonism to compensation has grown with experience. And in certain cases the licensing courts have used the power which they possess to issue colonial wine licences for public-houses closed by the popular vote, and in respect of which compensation had been paid. Wine shops are generally the worst class of drink shops; so that the last state of these houses has become worse than the first: for these, and other reasons, the above-mentioned resolution has been adopted.

"In future we shall concentrate our efforts on securing the direct veto without compensation. To this end we are about to secure the introduction of a Bill in Parliament. It will provide for a vote in each electoral district in conjunction with a general election, which takes place at least every three years, on the simple issue of prohibition. Each electoral district to decide the matter for itself. The prohibition would apply to the manufacture as well as the sale of intoxicants. A distinctive feature of the Bill is that it will provide for all women voting upon this question equally with all men. It, of course, provides for the repeal of compensation."

Queensland.—Queensland has the most simple and thorough-going Local Option Act of any of the southern colonies. By this Act, which was carried in 1885, one-sixth of the electors in a place can cause a direct vote to be taken on one or all of three propositions : (1) that the sale of intoxicating liquors shall be prohibited ; (2) that the number of licences shall be reduced to a certain number, not being less than two-thirds of the existing number ; (3) that no new licences shall be granted. The Act requires a two-thirds majority to carry the first proposition, but the second and third are carried by a simple majority. In over eighty per cent. of the elections held for the purpose of voting new licences, the temperance party has won. Very few attempts have been made to secure prohibition, and none of them have been successful : in a few cases, however, the people have decided in favour of reduction. The experience of Queensland seems to point to the conclusion that in a community where prohibitionists are not very strong (as in England) a provision giving the people power of preventing the issuance of new licences will do more good than placing in their hands the option of prohibition which they will not use.

In Queensland children under fourteen may not be served with liquor even to take away, and persons under eighteen may not be served for consumption on the premises.

New South Wales.—The present liquor law of New South Wales was carried by Sir Henry Parkes in 1881, and came into force at the beginning of 1882. The power of granting licences is placed in the hands of stipendiary magistrates specially appointed by the Government, and several restrictions are placed around the trade. The people are given a limited local option as to whether they will have new licensed houses or not. Polls take place on this question once every three years, at the same time as the municipal elections. The popular veto only applies to small houses however, and hotels with over twenty rooms can be licensed whether the people wish it or not.

There has been a strong movement throughout the colony for a more complete measure of local option, and several times within the last few years it has seemed as though this would be carried. The one difficulty in the way is the question of compensation ; and if the temperance party would only consent to recompensing dispossessed publicans, local option could be passed into law almost at once.

The temperance party itself in New South Wales has recently become divided. One section, consisting principally of the Good Templars, has wearied of seeking for local option, and declares that it will accept nothing less than State prohibition. Many of these irreconcilables are loud in their declarations that the great mass of teetotalers who are content to work for local option are little better than enemies of the cause. The only outcome of this split is likely to be the delay of temperance legislation of any kind there.

PART III.

THE CONTINENT OF EUROPE.

CHAPTER I.

THE STATE AS DISTILLER.

WHY should the trade in intoxicants be placed under special restraints? is the question sometimes asked; and the querists are hardly satisfied with the answer that it has continually been proved necessary, by the experience of all civilised Governments, to place limits on every business that is shown to be injurious to the well-being of the people. The drink traffic is admittedly such; therefore it has to be dealt with in a way quite different from the trades of the grocer or the baker. There are those who would have us believe that these very restrictions promote intemperance; and visionaries have more than once stated that the best way to encourage sobriety and to restrain excess would be to make the traffic absolutely free. The whole theory of Government is against such an idea. It is an axiom of statesmanship that to check any trade by legislation is to injure it; and that, within certain limits, the more severe the restrictions imposed on it, the less likely is a trade to thrive. But for answer to free-trade theorists we need not appeal to axioms of Government. The universal experience of nations goes to show that to allow the free manufacture and sale of intoxicants is to use the surest means of promoting all manner of excess. The official returns of France, Belgium and Germany within the last few years, all show that free trade in drink in these countries has proved an utter failure; and that under it, poverty, insanity and crime are increasing with terrible rapidity. Another remarkable illustration of this is to be found in the recent experience of Switzerland.

By article thirty-one of the Swiss Constitution of 1874 freedom of trade is specially guaranteed. The same year as the new Constitution was approved, the canton of Argovie wanted to know if this clause would prevent it limiting the number of drink shops in its borders. The Federal Council replied that "the limitation of the number of drink shops is no longer possible, on account of the principle of liberty of commerce and of industry imposed by article thirty-one of the Constitution".

The result was an immediate and considerable increase in the number of cabarets in nearly every canton. From 1870 to 1880 the total of these establishments was raised by 22 per cent., and in Geneva there was a wine shop for every 70 people, the average for the whole country being one drink shop for every 130 inhabitants. The effects of this on the condition of the people were immediately apparent. The French have a saying "to smoke and to drink like a Swiss, and to get tipsy like a Pole"; but now the Swiss, never the most temperate

8

nation, showed signs of rapid deterioration through intemperance. At the recruitment of 1880 the Medical
Commission reported that the number of young men
found fit for military service was from 5 to 25 per
cent. less than in 1873, and in some parts the
number of men fit for service was as low as 21·2 per
cent. The Principal Medical Officer declared that the
physical degeneration of the candidates was due to the
evil effects of spirit drinking and drunkenness. The
director of the Central Bureau of Charity stated that
80 per cent. of the applications of mothers and children
for relief were brought about by the tippling of the father
of the family. Sociologists pointed out that the nation
was rapidly being destroyed by this one curse; and in
order to obtain fuller details the Federal Assembly requested the Federal Council to make an inquiry into the
matter. The report of the latter body, when issued,
more than bore out the gloomy prognostications of the
alarmists. From 1877 to 1881, 3285 patients were
admitted to the public lunatic asylums, and of these
923 were brought there by alcoholism. There were
254 deaths annually directly caused by excessive drinking. Out of 2560 prisoners in cantonal penitentiaries,
1030 were found to be drunkards; and in eight re-
formatories 50 per cent. of the boys and 45 per cent.
of the girls were found to be the children of parents
one or both of whom were given to intoxication. In
Switzerland there are a larger proportion of suicides than
in any other civilised country, and the Commission found

that this was caused mainly by alcoholism. The Federal Council attributed the state of affairs to two reasons: (1) to the change in the economic condition of Switzerland owing to the introduction of railways; (2) partly to the fact that wine had become costly and inaccessible to the workmen, while at the same time spirits had become cheaper. Brandy was not only imported in great quantities from Germany, but was also manufactured on a large scale in industrial and domestic distilleries in Switzerland. The product of these small distilleries was specially dangerous, not only because of the alcohol it contained, but because of the crude and imperfect state of most of it. There was said to be between five and ten thousand domestic distilleries in the canton of Berne alone. To these causes, rather than to the increase of the shops for the sale of liquor, the Council attributed the increased alcoholism; but the popular opinion was against it on this point, and power was almost immediately afterwards given to the cantons to limit the number of public-houses. The chief recommendation of the Council was that steps should be taken to cheapen the price of beer and wine and to make spirits dearer.

In order to accomplish this latter aim the Government caused a popular vote to be taken on the question whether the Constitution should be so altered as to permit the traffic in intoxicants to be subject to control. There was a two-thirds majority in favour of control, and soon afterwards a scheme was formulated for making the manufacture of spirits entirely a State monopoly. This plan was started partly in the hope of checking drunken-ness and providing the people with pure drink; but undoubtedly a cause that was very largely responsible for its initiation was the hope of securing an abundant revenue.

Has the monopoly law been a success? Financially, yes; so far as ensuring the purity of the spirits sold, also yes; but for checking the consumption of strong drink it has been almost if not quite a failure. In saying this I am well aware that I express an opinion different from that of nearly every English writer on the subject, official and otherwise. Some at least of the data on which English writers have founded favourable opinions is partly unreliable and partly misleading. Thus in the (English) Foreign Office Report on Switzerland (No. 939) it was stated that the consumption of spirits in 1885, before the passing of the measure, amounted to 10·26 litres per head, and that this has been reduced by the monopoly to a little over 6 litres. Now it is impossible to say exactly what was the average consumption in 1885; but the monopoly itself, in its official returns, places the amount drunk per head that year, not at 10·26 litres, but at 7·25. The difference is enormous, and it must be remembered that it is rather to the interest of the monopoly to overstate than to understate the quantity drunk before it took over control. Moreover, from the figures for 1885 a by no means negligable amount must be deducted for that which, though reckoned in the

Swiss drink bill, was not consumed there but was smuggled to neighbouring countries.

For the first year there was a great decrease. The total spirit drinking, including that illegally obtained, was officially estimated at 5·50 litres per head, or less by one-quarter than in 1885. This was due principally to the rise in price of brandy. But since that year the total spirit bill has been steadily increasing. In 1890 it was 6·27 litres a head, in 1891, 6·32 litres, and in 1892 (the last year for which returns are available), 6·39 litres. These figures include only the amount sold through the monopoly. To them must be added three unknown quantities,—first, the spirits made by the people at their own homes from fruit; secondly, a proportion of the amount sold by the monopoly for use in manufactures, etc., and mixed with special preparations to render it undrinkable, which is admittedly often so doctored by people of depraved tastes as to be made potable again; and, thirdly, the amount smuggled. Formerly, as was said, Swiss spirits used to be smuggled into neighbouring countries; but now, owing to the rise in prices through the monopoly, drink from other countries is smuggled into Switzerland.

Those who claim for the State distilleries that they are potent forces in reducing the traffic in distilled liquors seem to mistake altogether their methods of working. The check to drunkenness has been produced, not by the State manufacturing drink, but by the prohibition of home manufacture and the increase in the price of spirits. It is no longer possible now for the peasant woman to manufacture her fiery draught from potatoes. and to feed her little one on it in place of milk. The distilleries are not managed so as to check drinking (for with that they have nothing to do), but to supply the dealers with pure liquors. In fact, it is to be expected that people who can afford it will now drink more spirits than they once would. Before the monopoly, much of the brandy was crude, of bad quality, and most injurious. Now it is purified and excellent; and, while I cannot claim to be an authority on this point myself, I am informed by persons who do drink that they can consume much more of properly prepared spirits than they can of those that contain any quantity of fusel oil and other harmful substances.

There were 1400 distilleries (besides the domestic stills) at the time the new plan was started; but these were all closed, with the exception of about three, compensation being paid to the owners. The establishments permitted to continue business are compelled to sell all their raw spirit to the Régie at a fixed rate; and in order to protect home trade the Régie is obliged to buy at least one-fourth of its spirits from native producers. No spirits can be imported by private individuals from foreign countries, except under strict conditions, and after a special tax has been paid on them. The monopoly minutely examines all liquor purchased by it; its purity is carefully ascertained, and then it is resold to retail dealers, either in the form of raw spirit or refined and prepared with a bouquet to suit the public taste. The prices fixed by the Régie are by no means high, but they are a decided increase on what were formerly charged. With this system of regulating the supply of spirits another was adopted at the same time of encouraging the consumption of beer and wine. The taxes on these drinks were remitted, and their sale made as free as possible from restriction. It was hoped that this would cause the people to use lighter drinks more ; and though it has made little difference to the wine trade, it has greatly helped to increase the popularity of beer.

Turning to the financial side of the business, the figures are almost enough to make any Chancellor of the Exchequer whose Budget shows a balance on the wrong side, become his own distiller. From June, 1887 (when the monopoly was started), till the end of 1888, the income was £492,944, the expenditure £294,631, and the profit remaining £198,313. In 1890 the income had reached £575,461, while the expenditure was £308,976, and the profit £266,485. For 1892 there was a still further all-round increase. The income was £591,470, the expenditure £360,321, and the profit £271,149. A portion of the profits has to be put on one side each year to repay the preliminary outlay of purchasing plant and compensating the old distillers. This cost £236,000, and it will be all paid off by 1898. A further sum has for a few years to be paid to several cantons in place of former revenues stopped by the creation of the monopoly ; and what remains is used for public purposes. Although the Régie is entirely under the control of the Federal Government, the latter does not take any of these profits, but they are distributed among the cantons in proportion to their population, and used by them as ordinary cantonal revenue.

One curious provision in the monopoly law is the stipulation that each canton shall devote one-tenth of the alcohol revenue for the purpose of promoting temperance. This vague provision has been interpreted by different bodies in various ways. In some parts the money is used for the relief of the poor, the maintenance of lunatic asylums, and the like; but there is growing up a strong conviction that it ought to be expended in more strictly temperance work, such as the financing of temperance societies, the cure and care of drunkards, and the instruction of children in the physiological effects of alcohol. By "temperance" the Swiss do not mean teetotalism, for total abstinence societies are almost unknown among them, the only one of any size being that of La Croix Bleue, which numbers some 4107 members and 2683 adherents.

The monopoly is in many ways useful; and, if people must drink spirits, there seems no reason why the State should not profit from their folly by itself securing the immense gain that accrues to the manufacturer. But it is a misnomer to call it a temperance agency; for it is no such thing. If Switzerland is ever to shake off the curse of intemperance which is still on it, its people must take some more active steps against it. Many of them are already realising this; and total abstinence societies, such as that of La Croix Bleue, are gradually spreading among its more thoughtful people. Strange to say, the first advocates of total abstinence in Switzerland were not so much the moral reformers who have adopted this as their own in other lands, as scientific men, who were led by their investigations to a firm conviction of the harmfulness and uselessness of alcohol. Religious and social reformers are now taking it up; but they are as yet a very small band, and they will need to do much before their cause makes much progress in Helvetia.

CHAPTER II.

THE GOTHENBURG SYSTEM.

THE Scandinavian licensing system has, during the last few years, received considerable attention from reformers in many lands; and rightly so. Whatever may be its faults, there is probably no other plan of liquor legislation of which it can be said that it has, in a comparatively short time, reduced the traffic in spirits by about three-quarters, without seriously discommoding the moderate drinkers, and without creating any illegal trade worth mentioning. There seems every likelihood that the system will, in a few years, spread far beyond the land of its inception. It satisfies the demand for increased State control, promises abundant revenue, and yet discourages the sale of liquor. A small body of public men in England are eager to have it adopted here; and acute observers in America declare that (provided no clauses in the State Constitutions are held to render it unlawful) it is almost certain to be tried there before long. A Bill has already been brought before the Massachusetts Legislature for the purpose of permitting such a trial, and has met with the approval of a considerable section of the people.

Less than half a century ago, Sweden was the most

drunken civilised country in the world. Its laws permitted almost free trade in the manufacture and sale of
spirits, and even the poorest peasants could obtain as
much brandy as they wanted. All the horrors that ever
follow habitual intemperance were to be seen throughout
the land. The poverty of the people was great; social
and moral degradation were prevalent; insanity and
crime were dangerously on the increase; and there was a
general air of hopeless desolation over the country. The
average consumption of spirits has been variously estimated at from a little under six to ten gallons per head
yearly; and the stuff, being home-manufactured, was of
the crudest and most injurious quality.

Patriotic Swedes soon began to look about for a
remedy for the national curse. Dr. Weiselgren commenced a crusade against spirit-drinking with most
remarkable results; and before long a hundred thousand
persons had enlisted themselves under his banner in a
league voluntarily abstaining from spirits. A still more
general movement shortly afterwards took place, when
people from all parts of the country petitioned Parliament to take some steps to check intemperance. In
response, a law was passed in 1855 abolishing domestic
and small stills, and giving rural localities the control of
the traffic, and the option of either having drink shops,
or sweeping them away altogether. Where it was decided
to still permit the sale of drink, the local authorities were
authorised to limit the hours of sale, and the number of
public-houses.

The people at once made considerable use of their newly acquired powers. There had been over 33,000 distilleries in 1853; the same year as the Act passed they were reduced to between 3000 and 4000. The greater number of country districts elected to go under complete prohibition; and whereas formerly spirits could be bought in nearly every peasant's house, there were now in the country districts less than 600 retail licences. The wholesale trade was not dealt with by the law.

There were no two opinions as to the beneficial effects of the new measure in the country; but it was found that the towns did not share equally in these benefits. It had been considered inadvisable to extend the option of prohibition to towns, and before long the great mass of public-houses became centred in urban districts. In 1856, though the towns contained only twelve per cent. of the people, three-quarters of the total public-houses were to be found in them, and eight townsmen were convicted of drunkenness to every one countryman.

The knowledge of these facts stirred the authorities up to see if nothing more could be done. In 1865 the Municipal Council of Gothenburg appointed a committee to inquire into the causes of pauperism. The committee reported that, "The worst enemy of the morals and well-being of the working classes in this community is brandy. Yet it is not the intoxicating liquor only and its moderate consumption which cause demoralisation and poverty; it is the disorder, evil example, temptations, and opportunities for every kind of iniquity with which public-house life abounds, that contribute mainly to this unhappy state of things. Neither local enactments nor police surveillance can do much so long as public-houses are in the hands of private individuals, who find their profit in encouraging intemperance, without regard for age or youth, rich or poor."[1] The committee recommended that the trade should be taken out of the control of the publicans, and managed by a company for the good of the community. A philanthropic company was formed, in consequence of this report, by a score of the leading inhabitants of the place, for the purpose of taking over the trade. It was specially stipulated that neither shareholders nor managers should be pecuniarily interested in pushing the sales, and the company was to receive no profits except 6 per cent. on the paid-up capital, all receipts beyond this going to the town treasury. The amount of paid-up capital required has been under £7000.

The company commenced its work on 1st October, 1865; and the way it has since fulfilled its obligations is worthy of the highest praise. It has shown an honest desire to carry out the sale of spirits in such a way as, while meeting the legitimate wants of the moderate

[1] This translation is taken from the Special Report of the United States Commissioner of Labour on *The Gothenburg System of Liquor Traffic*, Washington, 1893. I would here acknowledge my very deep indebtedness to this volume for many of the statistics contained in this chapter. Dr. Gould's work is unquestionably the fullest and most accurate book on the subject in the English language, or, as far as I am aware, in any other.

drinkers, shall discourage excess in every possible way. It has consistently attempted to restrict rather than to encourage the trade in liquor. The magistrates have granted it sixty-one licences, but of these it only uses nineteen (although the population of the place is considerably over a hundred thousand) and allows the remainder to lie in abeyance. The law permits public-houses to be open till 10 at night, but the company closes its establishments at from 7·30 to 9 o'clock, according to the season of the year. It has opened five coffee-houses and reading-rooms, where no spirits are sold, and four eating-houses, where none are obtainable except the customary dram at meals. Generally it has shown a wise and patriotic disregard of that policy which would sacrifice everything for a favourable balance sheet.

Each public-house is placed under the charge of a manager, who is expressly ordered not to encourage drinking in any way, and is warned that if he does so he will be dismissed. The company at first employed several of the old licensed victuallers and barmen; but before long it had to get rid of all of them, for they were so accustomed to encouraging tippling among their customers that they could not understand a system which forbade their doing it. The managers derive no direct or indirect profits from the sale of spirits beyond their stated salaries; and they have directions not to supply strong drink to young people, to those who show any signs of intoxication, or to those who require several drams in succession, or who pay repeated visits to the

public-houses at short intervals for the purpose of drinking. They are not allowed to give any credit for liquor.
Besides selling drink, each house has to keep a supply
of good hot and cold food, temperance drinks, cigars,
and the like. Inspectors are appointed whose sole duty
is to see that the managers conduct the trade properly.

The four eating-houses at which spirits are sold only
with meals are large, well conducted, and very popular.
They cater almost exclusively for working men, and sell
food at rates which put to shame even our own Lock-
harts and Pearces. A dinner of a large slice of pork, a
sausage, four potatoes and gravy, costs under twopence
halfpenny. When these houses were first opened nearly
every customer took a dram with his meals, but now
not more than half of them do so. The eating-houses
do not quite pay their way, but are run at a loss of a
little over £200 a year. The company regards the
money as well spent, for the places have a most beneficial
effect in promoting temperance. The five free reading-
rooms maintained by the company, in which no intoxicants (except small beer) are sold, cost between £600
and £700 a year to maintain. They are well supplied
with papers and books, and visitors can obtain light
refreshments of various kinds.

In considering the effects of the Gothenburg system
on the lives of the people, these two things must be
borne in mind : First, the system only touches the trade
in spirits, and has nothing to do with the sale of beer.
This latter is almost free, and has been rather encouraged

by the authorities than otherwise, under the mistaken notion that it would lessen the demand for stronger drink. Of wine and beer shops, licensed for consumption on the premises, there are 128, besides an unlimited number for consumption off the premises, requiring no licences. A large amount of the drunkenness in Gothenburg is caused by these beer shops. The police there ascertain, when a person is arrested for drunkenness, where he obtained his liquor; and from their returns it can be seen that the intoxication produced by beer is steadily increasing. In 1875 the number of persons arrested who drank last at beer saloons was 130; by 1885 the number had increased to 483; and in 1889 the number was 753.

A second important consideration in estimating the results of the system is the fact that even the whole trade in spirits is not in the hands of the company. There are seventeen restaurants, licensed by permission of the company, and managed by private individuals, which sell intoxicants. There are also five public-houses whose owners have the ancient right of carrying on the business, and with whom the company cannot interfere. Last of all, there are twenty-three wine merchants, who take out expensive licences from the company, for the sale of spirits off the premises.

Whatever deductions are drawn from the condition of the town as to the results of the system, considerable allowance must be made for the fact that the whole of the liquor traffic is not conducted by the company.

Perhaps the most outstanding evidence in favour of the system is this, that, not only are the people of the place well satisfied with it, but seventy-six other towns in Sweden have been led by it to adopt the same plan, and only thirteen places still retain the old method of selling the licences to private bidders. In Norway, too, the spirit trade is now conducted in nearly every town in substantially a similar way.

In discussing the effects of any liquor law it is never an easy task to decide how far social changes or effects are the cause of it, or how far they are due to other and entirely different economic causes. Immediately after the establishment of the company there was a great decrease in the consumption of drink and its attendant evils in Gothenburg; but this was due quite as much to the depression of trade as to anything else. Afterwards there was an increase of drinking, for trade greatly improved. It would be inaccurate either to wholly lay the cause of the decrease to the credit of the company or to blame it for the increase.

The following returns show the amount of drunkenness in Gothenburg during a few selected years :—

Year.	Population.	Arrests for Drunkenness.	
		Total.	Percentage.
1855	44,804	3431	13·8
1865	45,750	2070	4·5
1875	59,986	2490	4·2
1885	84,450	2475	2·9
1891	104,215	4624	4·4
1892	106,356	4563	4·3

It is not possible to give any reliable returns as to the amount of spirits consumed in Gothenburg. The sales of the company only represent part of the total quantity sold in the place, and all that the company sells is not consumed there. Much of it is bought by country people, who take it back with them to their own homes. The returns of the company show a fairly steady decrease. Thus in 1874-5 the total sales amounted to 29 quarts per head; in 1884-5, 19·1 quarts; and in 1891-2, only 14·3 quarts.

Financially, the company has from the first been a great success. It need not have ever called up a penny of its capital, had not the law required this to be done; and every year it has been able to hand over a very large surplus to the town, to be used for public purposes. In 1892 (the last year for which, at the time of writing, returns are available) the amounts paid to the city treasury were: (1) fixed fee for bar trade and retail licences, £15,632; (2) surplus profits, after paying all expenses, £21,868, or a total of £37,500. This amounted to the equivalent of over 7s. a head for every man, woman and child in the place. Formerly the city retained the whole of the surplus profits for its own benefit; but this created considerable dissatisfaction, and at last an alteration was made by which the municipality now only receives seven-tenths, the national treasury appropriating two-tenths, and the remaining tenth going to the country districts.

In Gothenburg the whole of the amount received by

the municipality goes for the relief of local taxation. This has been felt by many to embody a dangerous principle, as giving the city authorities a direct interest in the encouragement of drinking. To avoid this, the plan has been adopted in Norway of devoting the surplus, not to relieving the rates, but to helping charitable and philanthropic non-rate-aided enterprises.

The most notable example of the Norwegian plan is the town of Bergen. A liquor company was formed here in 1876, at the suggestion of the local magistracy, and it commenced business at the beginning of 1877. Not only is the distribution of profits here different, but the management of the houses varies too. In Gothenburg the aim has been to make the dram shops comfortable and attractive; in Bergen, on the contrary, the aim has apparently been to render them as uncomfortable and as repulsive as possible. Each house consists solely of a bar for the sale of liquor; nothing but liquor is sold, and when a person has consumed what he ordered he must go. No seats are provided, and customers are forbidden to loiter about the premises. This sternly repressive policy does not seem to have had a remarkable effect on the consumption of spirits; for whereas in 1877 the average sales per head came to 7·1 quarts, they were only reduced to 6·1 quarts in 1891; and this notwithstanding the fact that the average consumption for the whole of the country had been reduced in the same time from 6·3 quarts to 3·3 quarts. The number of arrests for drunkenness in Bergen in 1877 and 1891 was about the same; but a largely increased population in the latter year makes this show that the proportionate intoxication was really less. From the time of its commencement up to 1890, the Bergen company was able to distribute £69,731 among local philanthropic societies, and the recipients of its bounty have included all kinds of works for the common weal, museums, training ships, hospitals, a rescue society, orphanages, a tree-planting society, a fund for sea baths for the poor, temperance organisations, and the like. The profits which would otherwise have gone to enrich a few have thus been scattered about doing good to the many.

PART IV

ENGLAND.

CHAPTER I.

THE GROWTH OF THE LICENSING SYSTEM.

THE English are often said to be the most drunken among civilised nations ; but, like many other constantly repeated statements, this is not correct. Denmark, Belgium and Russia certainly take the precedence of us in this matter ; and it is an open question if alcoholism is not doing at least as much harm in northern and central France and Switzerland, as in the British Isles. The casual visitor to our lively neighbour sees but little open intoxication, and consequently assumes that France is a sober country. But those who have gone beneath the surface, and examined the results as recorded in the statistics of prisons and asylums, know that intemperance is rapidly becoming a national plague there.

While we may not be the worst offenders in this respect, it is yet undoubted that alcoholism is the greatest source of social misery in our land. Theorists may quarrel among themselves as to the exact proportion of poverty and crime produced by intemperance ; but no thinking man who is not altogether shut out from association with his fellows can doubt the awful ravages it is producing. We do not require to have it proved to us by figures; we only need to open our eyes and to use such brain power as we may possess to have the proof forced on us. Among the fashionable rich, among the idle women of upper middle-class families, as well as in our slum population, intemperance is doing a work of destruction before which the results of the most fatal diseases seem hardly worth notice.

Most of us would gladly be optimists on this subject, if hard facts would only let us ; but it is useless to indulge in an idle optimism, which suffers us to do nothing when the need of our services is greatest. It is accepted by many as an undeniable fact that we are steadily becoming a more sober people; but, unfortunately, statistics do not bear out this view. In some ways temperance has made great advances. Drunkenness is no longer looked upon as an amiable weakness, but as a serious offence against society and against oneself. The days of the three-bottle men are over, let us hope never to return; and the incessant drinking among friends that was common not many years ago is now little seen. Over one-sixth of the people have entirely abandoned the use of strong drink ; everywhere active temperance societies are working hard to promote sobriety; the conditions of life have become infinitely brighter and easier for the great mass of wage earners ; education has become universal, and the sale of alcohol has been placed under greater restrictions. Yet, notwithstanding all this, the drink trade was never so strong as it is to-day. Within fifty years the amount spent on liquor has almost doubled; though the police rarely arrest a drunken person except when outrageously disorderly, nearly 200,000 men and women are brought before the magistrates each year for intoxication;[1] and the number of deaths caused through inebriety cannot be estimated at a lower figure than 40,000 a year.

The Saxon chronicles tell how Edgar the Peaceable, acting on the advice of Archbishop Dunstan, determined to do something to check that drunkenness which was, the same a thousand years ago as to-day, all too prevalent on this island. He reduced the number of ale houses

---

[1] It is well known that the number of arrests for drunkenness is no adequate guide to the amount of intoxication. Speaking in the House of Commons, 13th March, 1877, on this point, Mr. Chamberlain said: "I have come to the conclusion that for our purpose police statistics are no good at all. As an evidence of this I will mention something with which I am acquainted in Birmingham. On a certain Saturday the number of persons arrested for drunkenness and brought before the magistrates was said to be 29—that was the total number of drunken cases credited, or rather, as I should say, debited to the town, according to the police statistics. During three hours of that same Saturday night, thirty-five houses in different parts of the town, beer houses, spirit shops and shops of other descriptions, were watched by different persons appointed for the purpose; and these persons reported that during those three hours 9159 males and 5006 females came out of those shops; and, out of these numbers, of the male persons there were 622 drunk, and 176 females in the same state. There is a total of 798 drunken persons, alleged to have been seen coming out of 35 houses in three hours; while the police returns only reported 29 for the day."

to one in each village, and had pegs put in the drinking cup to mark the amount that any person might consume at one draught. These drinking cups held about a couple of quarts each; and, if tradition speaks truly, it was no uncommon thing for men to finish up the whole of this quantity without once taking their lips from the vessel. By the law of Edgar, eight pegs were placed in each cup, and heavy penalties were provided for any person who dared to drink further than from one peg to another at a time. Edgar's efforts were not crowned with much success. The law restricting the number of public-houses was not long observed; and the draught limit led, in the end, to an increase in the evil it was designed to check.

After this attempt the trade was allowed to go on almost without restriction till the end of the fifteenth century; but then the evils caused by it became too apparent to be longer passively borne. In the year 1494, power was given to any two justices of the peace to stop the common selling of ale; and fifty-eight years later, in the reign of Edward VI., a serious attempt was made to grapple with the trade. Parliament complained that "intolerable hurts and troubles to the commonwealth of this realm doth daily grow and increase through such abuses and disorders as are had and used in common ale houses or other houses called 'tippling houses';" and in order to check these evils it passed various laws for the regulation of public-houses. This act is the foundation of our present licensing laws, and the three

main lines which it laid down for the limitation of the
business have continued to be observed ever since.
These are: (1) that the retail trade in intoxicants is an
exceptional business, which the State can only permit
to be carried on by duly licensed persons; (2) that the
power of granting licences lies with the justices of the
peace; and (3) that the magistrates have power, when
they think fit, to take away such licences.

Notwithstanding this Act, the national drunkenness
showed no signs of decreasing; and when James I.
came to the throne fresh efforts were put forth to check
it. For many years past the inns had been steadily
changing their character; and from being places of rest
and refreshment for travellers they had become principally tippling houses. So a measure was passed "to
restrain the inordinate haunting and tippling in inns".
According to the preamble of the Act, "the ancient,
true and principal use of inns was for the receipt and
relief and lodging of wayfaring people travelling from
place to place; and for the supply of the wants of such
people as are not able by greater quantities to make
their provision of victuals; and not meant for the enter-
tainments and harbouring of lewd and idle people, to
spend and consume their time in lewd and drunken
manner ".

To prevent this improper use of the taverns, various
stringent regulations were made. No resident in the
district or city where any inn was situated was allowed
to remain drinking in it unless (1) he was invited by

and accompanied some traveller staying at the inn ; (2) he was a labourer, in which case he would be allowed to stay at the inn for an hour at dinner time ; (3) he was a lodger; or (4) unless he was there for some other urgent and necessary cause, allowed to be such by two magistrates. A ten-shilling fine, to go to the poor, was the punishment for breaking this law.

Two years later, a further Act was passed for the prevention of drunkenness. According to the preamble, "The loathsome and odious sin of drunkenness is of late grown into common use, being the root and foundation of many other enormous sins, as bloodshed, stabbing, murder, fornication, adultery, and such like, to the great dishonour of God and of our nation, the overthrow of many good arts and manual trades, the disabling of divers workmen, and the general impoverishing of many good subjects, abusively wasting the good creatures of God ". This time it was provided that any person found drunk should be fined five shillings, or confined in the stocks for six hours. In 1609 a further Act was passed dealing with the matter, in which it was admitted that no success had attended the former attempts. "Notwithstanding all laws and provisions already made, the inordinate vice of excessive drinking and drunkenness doth more and more prevail." In order to more effectually suppress it, heavier penalties were provided, the landlord who permitted tippling was to lose his licence, and less evidence was required to secure a conviction. Not long afterwards the penalties were again increased.

It is notorious that all these measures failed to effect
their purpose. But the country was soon to learn that
difficult as it may be to promote sobriety by law, it is
easy enough for Parliament to encourage and promote
drunkenness. Soon after William and Mary came to the
throne, the nominal policy of previous reigns was altered,
with immediate and overwhelming results. Formerly
almost all the spirits used in England had been imported
from the continent, and the conditions under which
their manufacture could be carried on at home were such
as to keep the business very small. But in 1689 Parliament changed this. The Government was in great need
of money to meet the plots of traitors at home and
carry on its campaigns abroad; and it was thought that a
considerable revenue might be obtained by encouraging
the home spirit trade. Accordingly, the importation of
distilled waters from foreign countries was prohibited,
and the right to manufacture them was thrown open to
all, subject merely to the payment of certain excise dues.
The natural consequence was that the price of spirits
fell so greatly as to place them within the reach of all
classes. Before long dram drinking had, to use the
expression of Lecky, "spread with the rapidity and the
virulence of an epidemic". The results of free trade in
drink were visible all over the land. Gin shops arose in
all directions in every large town; and in London there
were, outside the city and the borough, over 6000 spirit
dealers to a population of 700,000. In less than fifty
years the consumption of British spirits rose sevenfold;

and everywhere the same tale was heard of the ruin it was bringing on all classes. It was at this time that the gin dealers hung out signs announcing that customers could get drunk for a penny, dead drunk for twopence, and have straw to lie on for nothing. Nor was this a mere boast; for many of the innkeepers actually provided rooms whose floors were covered with straw on which the intoxicated customers could lie until they recovered consciousness.

Such a condition of affairs could not be long permitted to continue. Parliament, alarmed at the results proceeding from its own action, set about for a remedy. As a first step, dealers in spirits were compelled to obtain licences, like ale house keepers; an annual charge of £20 was placed on the spirit licence, and the principle was introduced of having the licences renewed annually. But the change was made too suddenly, and the licence fee was too high; and this resulted in an extensive illicit trade springing up. In order to stop this, Parliament repealed the Act and passed another, forbidding the sale of spirits except in a dwelling-house, under a penalty of £10. That is to say, every householder was given leave to sell drink in his own home.

The last state was worse than the first. In 1736 the magistrates of Middlesex petitioned Parliament, stating forcibly the terrible results from the state of the law. A Parliamentary Committee was appointed to consider the whole matter; and it reported that the low price of spirituous liquors was the principal inducement to their excessive use ; and that, in order to prevent this, a duty should be placed on strong drink, and the right to vend it should be restricted. The same year the Government passed the famous Gin Act, a measure so stringent as to practically prohibit the sale of spirits. No person was allowed to dispose of them unless he had paid an annual licensing fee of £50; and the penalty for breaking the law was a fine of £100. A tax of twenty shillings a gallon was also placed on all spirits manufactured.

The Gin Act came too late. The passion for spirits had become firmly rooted among the people, and they would not consent to have their supplies cut off. They rose against the officers appointed to carry out the Act, and in many of the larger towns there was for some time danger of rebellion. The legal sale of proof spirits dropped in a year to two-thirds of its former proportions; but an immense illicit trade was carried on, which far more than balanced the reduction. All the power at the back of the Government was not enough to obtain the enforcement of this measure, though the magistrates made strenuous efforts to carry it out. In two years 12,000 persons were convicted of breaking the law, but all the prisons of the country would have failed to hold a tithe of those who openly set it at defiance. The excise officers were held in general detestation, and informers or any who dared to appear in excise prosecutions went in danger of their lives. At last the Government had to give way, and in 1742 the Act was repealed.

In 1828 the various Acts relating to the licensing of

public-houses were consolidated, and the control of them was made more stringent. Two years later a new and most unfortunate departure was taken. With the hope of causing people to abandon the drinking of spirits, Parliament determined to encourage the sale of beer; and an Act was passed permitting any householder to open a beer shop on paying an excise fee of two guineas. The consumption of beer rose twenty-eight per cent. in consequence; but it was soon found that this, in place of checking the rush to spirits, aided it; and the increase in the spirit trade was even greater than that in beer. The number of houses for the sale of intoxicating liquors rose from 88,930 to 123,396; and many old inns, that formerly had been respectably conducted, were now driven by the stress of competition to very doubtful means for the promotion of their trade. At the same time crime showed a great increase, and, to quote from a Report of a Committee of the House of Lords, "The commitments for trial in England and Wales in the years 1848-49 were, in the proportion to those of 1830-31, the two first years after the enactment of the Beer Act, of 156 to 100; that this is not a mere casual coincidence the Committee have the strongest reasons to believe from the general evidence submitted to them, but more especially from that of the chief constables of police and the chaplains of gaols, who have the best opportunities, the one of watching the character of the beer shops and of those who frequent them, the other of tracing the causes of crime and the career of criminals".

The Report of a Committee of the House of Commons in 1854 was still more emphatic. "The beer shop *h* system," it said truly, "has proved a failure."

Off Licences.—Through legislation introduced by Mr. Gladstone early in the "sixties," persons are now permitted to sell spirits, wine or beer in bottles, for consumption off the premises, on payment of a small licence fee. Previous to then it was illegal for any spirit merchant to supply less than two gallons at a time. The new law has led to a considerable trade in strong drink through grocers, and it has been estimated that the off licence holders supply about five per cent. of spirits sold. This departure has been the object of very considerable opposition from both publicans and temperance advocates. The publicans naturally object to having a large part of what was their monopoly thrown open to almost free competition; and temperance advocates declare that the off licences are very largely responsible for the rapid increase of intemperance among women. It is said that many who would not venture to go to a public-house to order what they want, quietly and secretly obtain their supplies through the grocer, and are able to indulge at home without restraint. Innumerable clergymen and doctors declare that, to their personal knowledge, these facilities have largely promoted female intemperance. But in the very nature of the thing, these statements, while worthy of all attention, are not capable of ordinary proof. The only way they could be shown to be true would be by naming a large number of cases,

with names and addresses, and submitting them for
examination. Naturally neither clergymen nor doctors
can do this ; for it would be impossible for them to make
public the secrets of persons whose inner histories they
learn in their professional administrations. It was this
that caused the failure of the temperance party to convince the Committee of the House of Lords, in 1879,
as to the harmfulness of the off licences. In its Report,
the Lords' Committee made this statement about the
matter :—

"The question which the Committee have had to consider is, not whether some cases of intemperance may be
traced to the purchase of spirits at grocers' shops, but
whether any general increase of intemperance can be
attributed to grocers' licences. After the examination of
many witnesses on the point, and after the best inquiries
they could make, the Committee have obtained very
little direct evidence in support of this view ; and the
conclusion they have come to is, that upon the whole
there have been no sufficient grounds shown for specially
connecting intemperance with the retail of spirits at
shops as contrasted with their retail at other licensed
houses."

Sunday Closing.—Sunday closing now prevails over
almost the whole of the empire, with the exception of
England itself. It is in force in nearly every colony,
and in Scotland, Wales and Ireland. For the latter
country an Act was passed in 1877, granting this measure
to the whole island, except Dublin, Cork, Belfast,

Limerick and Waterford, for the space of four years. The Act was looked upon as purely experimental; but it operated so successfully that it has since been renewed, year by year, as an annual measure. Many efforts have been made to place it on a permanent basis, and to include the five exempted cities in its scope. Both Protestants and Catholics are agreed as to its necessity, and leading statesmen of both parties have testified to its beneficial effects.

In 1888, when Mr. T. W. Russell brought before the House a Bill to make Sunday closing permanent and general in Ireland, the opponents of the measure obtained the appointment of a Committee to inquire into the results of the Act. After a most exhaustive inquiry this Committee reported in favour of it, and recommended—

(*a*) That all drink shops in Ireland close at nine P.M. on Saturdays.

(*b*) That the present Irish Sunday Closing Act be made permanent, and include the five hitherto exempted towns.

(*c*) That the distance requisite for a person to travel to qualify as a *bonâ-fide* traveller entitled to purchase refreshments be increased from three miles to six.

This was a great triumph for the Sunday closers. In the words of Mr. A. J. Balfour, "it was not unfair to say that the whole weight of evidence, with comparatively insignificant exceptions, was in favour of the continuance of Sunday closing in Ireland, and of the adoption of Saturday closing after nine o'clock. The people who

10

gave evidence were not drawn from one class of the community, but they represented every class and every section of opinion."

Since then Acts have been brought in year after year embodying these recommendations; but although supported by the Government it has never been found possible to carry them, chiefly on account of the congested condition of business in the Commons.

In Scotland Sunday closing has been in force under the "Forbes-Mackenzie Act" since 1854. It works on the whole very successfully, as might be expected from the fact that in all things Scotland is strongly a Sabbath-observing country. In Wales this law has also been in force since 1882. It is admitted to be a fair success in the interior of Wales; but great difficulty has been found in enforcing it in Cardiff, and along the border line between England and Wales. In Cardiff a very large shebeen trade has sprung up, and a number of clubs have been established for the avowed purpose of supplying their members with liquor on Sundays.

In 1889, in consequence of many statements that were in circulation declaring Sunday closing in Wales to be a failure, the Government appointed a Royal Commission, presided over by Lord Balfour of Burleigh, to inquire into the matter. To the great surprise of many, the Commission reported in favour of the Act, and declined to recommend either modification or repeal of it, stating that "a change in this direction would be unwelcome to a vast majority of the population".

CHAPTER II.

PLANS for the reform of the licensing laws are legion, and more Bills are brought before the House of Commons year by year dealing with this matter than with any other. To describe every one of these plans would be wearisome and useless. It will answer every purpose to confine this chapter to the chief measures proposed within this last quarter of a century.

MR. BRUCE'S BILL.—No more careful or more thorough attempt has been made to change the licensing laws than that introduced by Mr. Bruce (now Lord Aberdare), who, as Home Secretary to the Liberal Government, framed a Bill on the subject in 1871. In bringing it before the House of Commons he laid down five propositions, as leading principles which he thought might be expected to receive the assent of all the members. They were :—

1. That under the existing system of licensing, far more licences have been issued than are required by public convenience, there being one to every 182 people.

2. That the present mode of issuing licences is unsatisfactory, no guidance being given to the magistrates either as to the number to be issued or the respectability

(147)

and the responsibility of the persons seeking to be licensed.

3. That no sufficient guarantees are taken as to the orderly management of public-houses or their supervision.

4. That the laws against adulteration are insufficient, and, such as they are, are imperfectly enforced.

5. That the hours during which public-houses are allowed to be open admit of reduction without interfering with the liberty or the material convenience of the people generally.

To these he added two other propositions, on which he did not expect such unanimous agreement. (1) That the public have a right to be supplied with places of refreshment sufficient in number, convenient, and respectably conducted. (2) That all existing interests, however qualified the interests may be, are entitled to just and fair consideration.

On the basis of these propositions he built up a plan which still deserves the careful attention of all licensing reformers. The leading principles of it were as follows: The licensing powers were to still be retained by the magistrates, and no liquor licences were to be issued without their certificates. All old licences were to remain in force for ten years from the passing of the Act, as of right, and then they were to absolutely lapse. New licences were to be granted on a novel plan. The justices would meet together before the licensing day, and would decide on the number of new licences to be issued, altogether apart from the question of to whom they were to be given. If the number of public-houses in the neighbourhood, when the proposed new establishments had been added, did not exceed a certain fixed scale, then the decision of the magistrates would be final. If, however, the new licences would bring the total above that proportion, then it would be necessary to take a vote of the ratepayers as to whether the increase should be permitted or not, and the majority of those voting would decide. The scale was, in towns, one licensed house for 1500 people and under, two houses for up to 3000 people, and one more for every additional 1000 ; in the country, one licensed house for 900 people and under, two for up to 1200, three for up to 1800, and one more for every additional 600 inhabitants.

When the number of new licences to be issued had been fixed, they were to be put up to public auction, and sold to the highest bidders, one person having power to buy any number or all of them. The purchaser would be allowed to select his own house for carrying on the business, provided it was within the limits of the district ; but before receiving his licence he would have to obtain a certificate from the magistrates that the premises chosen were suitable for the purpose, and that the proposed manager was a proper person. It would not be necessary for the licence-holder to be his own manager. All licences so purchased were to be renewed annually, as of right, for ten years after the passing of the Act, except when forfeited by misconduct.

At the end of ten years, when all licences, old and new, were about to lapse, the magistrates would decide anew what the number of public-houses in their neighbourhood should be. If they decided to exceed the statutory limits, then it would be necessary to poll the ratepayers and obtain their sanction to the proposal; but if the number proposed by them was not in excess of those limits, then this need not be done. The licences would again be put up for sale for another ten years, and the same process would be repeated at the end of each decade. In the case of eating-houses and beer and wine licences for refreshment-rooms these regulations would not apply, but the magistrates might grant licences at their discretion. Nor would they apply to houses selling drink for consumption off the premises only; for these, the justices would grant certificates, on certain conditions being observed by the applicants.

The control of drink shops was to be made much stricter. A second conviction for serious breaches of the law would lead to forfeiture of the licences, without choice on the part of the magistrates. Every conviction must be recorded on the back of the licensing certificates; and on the police penalties for offences under the Act amounting in three consecutive years to £65, or in five years to £100, the licence would be taken away.

In order to secure the better enforcement of the law an entirely new body of inspectors was to be created. These should be quite independent of the local authorities, and their sole duty would consist of supervising the

liquor sellers. There was to be one inspector-in-chief;
England and Wales would be divided into counties
with an inspector for each, and every large town and
district would have a superintendent, under whom there
would be a carefully selected and well-paid body of men.
" The police cannot properly and ought not to be
entrusted within the walls of a public-house," Mr. Bruce
said. " It is utterly impracticable to have a proper
system of inspection if steps are not taken to make the
inspection more efficacious; and efficient inspection can
in my opinion be conducted only by a body of men
altogether independent of the police. . . . They will
be . . . specially charged with the duty of seeing that
no offence is committed in a public-house which is prohibited by law." The cost of this inspection was to be
defrayed from the licence fees.

Finally, the Bill contained clauses specially directed
against adulteration. Samples of the liquors sold were
to be frequently taken and analysed at Somerset House
laboratory. When it was found that any injurious in-
gredients had been mixed with them, the seller would be
liable, for a first offence, to a fine of £20 or imprisonment for one month, with or without hard labour; and,
for a second offence, to a fine of £100 or three months'
hard labour, and forfeiture of licence.

Mr. Bruce's proposals fell like a bomb among the
brewers and publicans. They realised that the time had
now come when they must fight for their very existence;
and fight they did. Temperance meetings were broken

up all over the country, every tap-room became the centre of a campaign against the Government, and all the liquor sellers and their adherents became unswerving Tories in a day. Intense pressure was brought to bear on individual members, and the Government became the object of most intense hostility. There was not, at that time, the strong sentiment throughout the country in favour of restrictive legislation which is to be found now; and every bar parlour was used as the head-quarters and meeting house of a propaganda to convince working men that the Bill was a measure aimed against the liberty of the people. The *Times*, to the surprise of many, gave Mr. Bruce its warmest support, and day by day did its best to strengthen the hands of the Government. The great body of middle-class people, too, were inclined to approve of the measure. But the forces against it were too strong; and after a few weeks the Ministry gave way, and it was announced that, owing to the time that had been wasted over the Budget, there would be no opportunity of proceeding with the measure that Session.

What were the teetotalers doing all this time? Where was the United Kingdom Alliance? Where were the hundred and one other bodies that had been clamouring for years for reform? Here was a Ministry that had been bold enough to risk office in order to promote temperance; surely it had a right to look to the temperance party for cordial support! If it looked, however, it looked in vain, for the influence of the teetotalers was worse than thrown away in this struggle. The United Kingdom Alliance was so busy promoting petitions in favour of a Permissive Bill which every one knew had no chance of success, that it had no energy to spare for helping on the Government. It officially announced that its attitude was one of " friendly neutrality"; and when the secretary of the Alliance was urged by the *Leeds Mercury* to support the Bill, he replied that " it (the drink trade) ought not to be sanctioned by law, nor tolerated within the range of Christian civilisation ".

No more suicidal policy, no course more fatal to the promotion of temperance in our land, could possibly have been taken. At a time when every publican and every brewer was seeking the destruction of the Government on account of its attitude to the drink question, the Alliance was content to be " friendly neutral " ! By their almost inexplicable conduct, the leaders of that body helped to delay temperance legislation for a quarter of a century, and created a deep distrust of teetotalers in the minds of most politicians. If they had actively thrown themselves into the breach, had used all their forces to support the Ministry, had been content to drop for a few months the plan of bringing forward a measure which they knew Parliament would certainly reject,—then Mr. Bruce and his colleagues might have been encouraged to proceed, and the liquor traffic in England would by this time have been cut down to a fraction of its old proportions.

Mr. Caine recently claimed that the temperance party

rather supported than opposed the Government at this crisis; and that, in fact, "practically, their only friends and supporters in the constituencies were the teetotalers". No one denies that many individual abstainers, as, for instance, Mr. Caine himself, were active in helping on the measure; but the temperance party as a whole was not. The month after the Bill was abandoned, Mr. Bruce publicly charged Sir Wilfrid Lawson, in the House of Commons, with having hindered and greatly diminished its chance of success by the course he had taken. While the Bill was still before the country, and while its fate was trembling in the balance, many prominent abstainers opposed it bitterly, and spoke and wrote against it. Professor Newman, in answer to a request from Mr. S. Morley, that he and his friends of the Alliance would not refuse an instalment because they did not get all they wanted, replied: "The United Kingdom Alliance cannot postpone its action for ten years. . . . Its (the Bill's) good points will not help us; they are not things which we asked; its evil points will damage us extremely. Hence if we fail to induce Mr. Bruce to withdraw his astonishing innovations of principle, I certainly do not guarantee that our friends will refrain from total opposition."

Mr. Raper, a leading temperance speaker, at a meeting in the Manchester Town Hall, held under the auspices of the United Kingdom Alliance, said: "It is strange that a man of such a powerful intellect as the Home Secretary should be so remarkably defective in observation of

a logical kind.   I have not seen a greater wonder this
quarter of a century than I did when I saw this able man
standing for two hours and ten minutes giving forth grand
principles and   then cutting them   to   pieces—making
statements which he followed up with nothing."

To judge from the speeches of Dr. F. R. Lees, who is
considered by many the premier writer on total abstinence, one would think that the Bill had been framed by
a committee of Burton brewers.   " Give no unwise and
blind support to the proposition of the Government," he
said.   " I do not think that the Bill, as a practical Bill, is
worth discussing in detail. . . . It is a wholesome and
righteous principle, that of public control over the liquor
traffic ; but you are denied your claim, it is postponed for
ten years, while the existing generation of victims shall
perish, and a new generation shall take their place."

Why rake up all these old mistakes ? it may be asked.
Why not forget the past?   The answer is plain.   The
old matter must be borne in mind, not in order to be-
little and denounce the men who made the mistakes, but
so that the reformers of the present may learn from the
blunders of their predecessors, and not again wreck the
ship because it is only sailing towards port with a couple
of sails instead of a full rig.

MR. CHAMBERLAIN'S PLAN.—In 1876 some stir was
made by Mr. Chamberlain advocating an adoption of the
Gothenburg system in England.   The Birmingham Town
Council expressed its approval of the plan; and on
13th March, 1877, Mr. Chamberlain brought forward a

resolution in the House of Commons: "That it is desirable to empower the Town Councils of boroughs, under the Municipal Corporation Acts, to acquire compulsorily, on payment of fair compensation, the existing interests in the retail sale of intoxicating drinks within their respective boroughs; and thereafter, if they see fit, to carry on the trade for the convenience of the inhabitants, but so that no individual shall have any interest in nor derive any profit from the sale".

This motion was supported by Sir Wilfrid Lawson and his allies; but was rejected by a large majority, 103 voting against and only 51 in its favour.

MR. RITCHIE'S LOCAL GOVERNMENT BILL.—In 1888, when the Local Government Bill was introduced by the Unionist Government, it contained clauses providing that the whole of the licensing of public-houses should be handed over to the County Councils; and that, in addition to the powers now held by the magistrates, the Councils should have authority to close the houses on Sunday, Good Friday and Christmas Day, either altogether or for part of the day, to alter the hour of closing at night, and to increase the licensing fees not more than 20 per cent. There were two great limits to the proposed power of the Councils. The first gave the magistrates power to prevent the renewal of a licence on proof that the holder was guilty of illegal conduct. The second limit was the provision that when the Councils refused the renewal of a licence for any other cause than the fault of the holder, the latter should be entitled to com-

pensation. Such compensation was to be assessed on
"the basis of the difference (if any) between the value of
the licensed premises immediately before the passing of
this Act and the value which such premises would have
then borne if the licence had then determined". The
compensation was to be divided between the persons
interested in the premises, either by agreement among
themselves, by arbitration, or, finally, by the County
Court. The cost of the compensation was to be borne
ordinarily by the licensing division of the county in which
the house was situated; or sometimes, under exceptional
circumstances, by the whole county.

The temperance party, although on the whole pre-
ferring *ad hoc* Boards, would gladly have accepted the
proposals, but for the compensation clauses. Over these
a hot fight was made, and innumerable meetings were
held all over the country against them. The licensed
victuallers were at first also inclined to oppose the measure; but they soon realised that it would be on the
whole a great gain to them. As Mr. Ritchie, the
father of the Bill, pointed out to a deputation, "We
practically give you a vested interest by the Bill". But
the opposition to the objectionable clauses was too
strong; and in June Mr. W. H. Smith announced, for
the Government, that the whole of the licensing section
would be withdrawn.

Mr. Goschen's Compensation Plan.—Two years
later a second attempt was made by the same Government to legalise compensation. In the *Local Taxation*

(*Customs and Excise*) *Bill* a scheme was formulated for the gradual reduction of public-houses. The main idea of this scheme was that each year the sum of £440,000, raised by increased taxes of 3d. a barrel on malt liquors and 6d. a gallon on spirits, should be used for the buying up of licences for the purpose of extinction. Of this sum, £350,000 was to go to England, £50,000 to Scotland and £40,000 to Ireland. In England and Scotland the money was to be apportioned among the County Councils, which would be·permitted to buy up such licensed premises as they thought proper; in Ireland the authority to be appointed was the National Debt Commissioners. No compulsory powers of purchase were given; but all purchases would have to be made by agreement with the owners of the houses, at prices and under conditions fixed by mutual arrangement. After the passing of the Act, no new licences, except for eating-houses and refreshment-rooms, were to be granted unless the consent of the County Councils had first been obtained, and even when new licences were granted, it was to be on the express understanding that their renewal might "at any time be refused at the free and unqualified discretion of the licensing authority".

In bringing the Bill before the House of Commons Mr. Ritchie said: " I assure the House that the sole object which the Government has in view is to promote temperance, and to help those who are endeavouring and who have so long endeavoured to battle against intemperance. . . . I have not the least intention of interfering with any powers now possessed by licensing magistrates. . . . Our sole object has been to help temperance reformers, and to promote the cause of temperance." But temperance reformers did not see the matter quite in the same light as Mr. Ritchie; and the opposition to the proposals of 1890 was even stronger than to those of 1888. The main objections were that the measure created a vested interest where none previously existed, and that the proposals for extinction were utterly and ridiculously inadequate. Mr. Caine, a prominent Liberal Unionist supporter of the Government, resigned his seat in Parliament as a protest against the scheme; and before many weeks had passed, the second attempt was sent the same way as the first. The money intended for the compensation of the publicans was devoted instead to technical education.

LORD RANDOLPH CHURCHILL'S BILL.—In the same month as the Local Taxation Bill was introduced, Lord Randolph brought before the House of Commons his scheme for amending the licensing laws. This plan was admittedly partly based on Mr. Bruce's Bill of 1871. The licensing authority was to be vested in the municipal authorities for boroughs and the County Council for counties. These bodies were not only to have the right to license, but also to regulate the hours of closing on Sundays and week-days. The power of direct veto was to be placed in the hands of the people, and in a parish where two-thirds of the ratepayers on the municipal rate book voted for prohibition, no licences were to be granted.

Beer shops were to be swept away, and the kinds of licences were to be reduced to two,—the full publican's licence and the refreshment-house wine and beer licence; and the rating qualification for a building used as a public-house was also to be considerably increased. Clubs in which drink was consumed were to be registered and to pay fees ranging from 30s. a year for a working men's club to from £1000 to £2000 for the great West-end clubs. The noble lord was strongly in favour of compensation, and declared: "I hold that compensation for vested interests is an indispensable accompaniment to any scheme of licensing reform. Any such reform not accompanied by compensation for vested interests would be sheer confiscation and robbery." But he did not deal with this detail in his Bill, on the ground that it would entail taxation in some form or another; and it is not in the power of a private member of Parliament to propose to the House taxation of any form or kind. Lord Randolph's measure met with a very favourable reception when introduced, but he did not proceed even to the second reading with it.

THE BISHOP OF CHESTER'S BILL.—In 1892, Dr. Jayne, Bishop of Chester, brought before the public a modification of the Gothenburg system that has since attracted a considerable amount of attention. He recognises that intemperance is far too common, and that our public-house system stands urgently in need of reform; but he believes that the use of alcoholic beverages must be accepted as inevitable, and that the best plan to adopt is not to seek to abolish the drink trade altogether, but to reform it. One of the great evils of the present system is that those who conduct public-houses have a direct pecuniary interest in selling the largest amount of drink possible; the Bishop desires to change the object of the sellers from private profit to the public welfare. To do this he would have philanthropic companies formed, which should buy up all the public-houses in a district, have a monopoly of sale, and conduct the traffic for the public welfare. The companies would derive no profit from the sale, except a certain fixed amount of interest on the capital invested. In their houses (to quote Dr. Jayne's own description) "alcoholic beverages, though frankly recognised, will be disposed from their aggressive supremacy, and supplied under less seductive conditions. These conditions would, for example, be comfortable, spacious, well-ventilated accommodation; temperance drinks brought well to the front, invested with prestige, and supplied in the most convenient, attractive and inexpensive way; the pecuniary interests of the managers (*e.g.,* in the form of bonus) made to depend entirely on the sale of eatables and non-alcoholic beverages; alcoholic liquors secured against adulteration; newspapers, indoor games, and, where practicable, out-door games and music, provided; while the mere drink shop, the gin palace, and 'the bar'—that pernicious incentive to drinking for drinking's sake — would be utterly abolished."

Dr. Jayne's first thought was that such houses might

be managed by the County Councils, but he soon saw
that it would be better to place them in the hands of
private companies. The methods by which he proposes
that the companies should set to work may be best seen
from an account given by him in the *Daily Graphic*
for 25th October, 1893: "We are prepared to under-
take the licensed victualling of your locality, paying to
the dispossessed publicans such compensation as law
and equity may require. We will at once reduce our
houses to such number as the licensing authority may
deem necessary; we will re-engage respectable publicans
as managers on terms far more favourable to themselves,
their families and the community, than managers now
enjoy under the tied-house system. They will receive a
fixed salary, with a bonus on the sale of eatables and
non-alcoholic drinkables, but with absolutely no benefit
from the sale of intoxicants. They will thus have no
inducement to push the sale of alcohol, to drink with
their customers, or to adulterate their liquors. As regards
hours of closing and details of management we shall,
within legal limits, be guided by local experience and
opinion. Our surplus profits will be applied to public,
non-rate-aided objects, including the establishment of
bright and attractive temperance houses, to which those
who wish to keep quite clear of the temptations of alcohol
in any shape may safely resort."

In 1893 he incorporated these proposals in a Bill
which he brought before the House of Lords. The
measure was defeated on the second reading; but Dr.

Jayne is still hopeful that Parliament will grant the necessary powers for the attempt to be made where desired. Would it not be better for some town to definitely decide to adopt the Gothenburg system, and then go to Parliament with a request for an authorisation to do so? Such a demand is far more likely to be granted than a proposal that may be adopted anywhere or nowhere. If the method proved a success when first tried, there would be little difficulty in obtaining permission for other places to follow suit.

THE BISHOP OF LONDON'S BILL.—*The Licensing Boards Bill* may be taken as representing the plans of a moderate school of reformers. It was framed under the supervision of the Church of England Temperance Society, and introduced into the House of Lords in 1893 by Dr. Temple, Bishop of London. The Church of England Temperance Society differs in many ways from most temperance organisations. Its social work is worthy of all praise, and its magnificent agencies for the rescue of criminals and inebriates are so well known as hardly to require mention. But in the matter of legislative action, this society does not take up the extreme attitude of such organisations as the United Kingdom Alliance. Its membership contains a very large, if not a predominating Conservative element; and hence its proposals deserve attention as being those of the members of a party usually not foremost in legislation of this kind.

The Bill brought forward by the Bishop of London in 1893 proposed to transfer the power of granting all drink, billiard, music and dancing licences from the justices in each district to a specially elected Licensing Board. The Board was to be elected triennially by persons on the local government register of electors, and the cost of such elections and other expenses of management were to be borne by the borough or County Council. The Board would have power to alter the hour of closing on week-days, and all licensed houses would be closed on Sunday unless by special order of the Board. Even when the Board sanctioned Sunday opening, the houses would only be permitted to remain open for two hours, and could only sell drink for consumption off the premises. All clubs would have to be registered, fees being payable for such registration; and power would be given to the police to enter any club which they had reason to believe was carried on simply as a drinking club, and to charge the members found on the premises and the owner of the house before a magistrate. The principal provisions of the Bill, however, would not come into effect until five years after the passing of the Bill, when a large reduction of licences would take place compulsorily. This five years' term of grace was provided for as a kind of compensation. At the end of five years from the passing of the Bill into law the following provisions would come into operation :—

> (*a*) The only licences that are to be granted are (i.) a full publican's licence; (ii.) a wine and beer on licence for a refreshment house; (iii.) a wine

and beer off licence; (iv.) a licence for an hotel; and (v.) a licence for a railway refreshment room, the two last being special forms of the publican's licence. After 1898, therefore, the following kinds of licence will cease to be obtainable : (i.) The beer dealer's additional licence (off) ; (ii.) the beer retailer's on and off licences ; (iii.) the cider and perry on and off licence ; (iv.) the table beer retailer's licence (off) ; (v.) the wine retailer's on and off licences ; and (vi.) the sweets retailer's on and off licences. None of these licences are required by a person holding a superior licence.

(*b*) The Board is to have full discretion to grant or not to grant any licence. After this provision comes into effect the present restrictions on the power to refuse certain licences, except on certain grounds, will cease.

(*c*) Licences, exclusive of hotels and railway refreshment rooms, are not to be granted in excess of a fixed proportion to the population of each district—one per 1000 in towns, one per 600 in country—but proper notice is to be given to a licence holder before discontinuing his licence under this clause.

(*d*) The value qualification of premises is raised.

(*e*) A licensed person is not to carry on any other retail business on the licensed premises.

The measure came before the House of Lords for its

second reading on the 12th May, 1893. It met with a
very unfavourable reception, and Lord Salisbury opposed
it hotly as being "the wrong remedy for the evil we all
deplore". At last Dr. Temple, seeing that it was perfectly evident the measure would be rejected by a considerable majority, consented to allow the motion to be
negatived without a division. It is the intention of the
Church of England Temperance Society, however, to
keep its Bill as far as possible to the front, and to make
persistent efforts to have it carried into law.

LOCAL OPTION.—Few schemes of reform have been so
unceasingly pushed as that for giving to localities the
option of prohibition. Forty years ago, when it was first
brought before the British public, it was laughed at, and
hardly deemed worthy of the serious notice of politicians;
in 1893 it was introduced by the Government to the
House of Commons; and to-day it has all the weight of
one of the two great political parties behind it. Whatever may be thought of the practical usefulness of such
an option in the present state of public opinion, it is
hardly possible to deny to the men who demand it a
tribute of admiration for their persistency and pluck.

On the 1st June, 1853, the United Kingdom Alliance
was founded for the purpose of securing "the total and
immediate legislative suppression of the liquor traffic".
Its plan of operations was to secure for any locality that
wishes it the right to prohibit the traffic in intoxicants
there. Eleven years after the formation of the Alliance
Sir W. Lawson introduced his famous Permissive Bill,

embodying the demands of the Alliance, to the House of Commons. It was defeated by a majority of over seven to one; but in 1869 the majority against it was reduced to a little over two to one. In 1879 Sir Wilfrid changed his tactics; and instead of incurring the cost of introducing a Bill year by year, he brought forward a resolution in favour of "some efficient measure of local option". In 1880, before a full House, the resolution was at last carried by a majority of 26; 245 voting for, and 219 against.

It was expected that the Liberal Government then in force would do something to carry the resolution into effect; but nothing was done until 1893, when Sir William Harcourt's much-debated Local Option Bill was introduced. The provisions of this Bill are very simple, and include two things,—the option of prohibition, and the option of Sunday closing. It provided that on one-tenth of the local government electors in any division making the request in writing, a poll shall be taken as to whether all public-houses be closed there, or whether there shall be Sunday closing. The latter proposal can be carried by a simple majority of those voting; but to secure entire prohibition there must be a majority of two-thirds. Whatever way the electors decide would remain in force for three years; but at the end of that time the question might be re-opened by a similar petition, and a fresh poll held. But when prohibition had been carried it could only be repealed by a two-third vote against it. The electoral areas were very small, each ward in a

borough divided into wards being a separate district.
No compensation was provided; but the clauses for prohibition were not to come into effect until three years
after the passing of the Act. The prohibition was not
to affect railway refreshment-rooms, hotels, or eating-
houses.

The Bill caused considerable excitement; but there
was a noticeable difference in its reception and in that
accorded to Mr. Bruce's Bill of 1871. In 1871 the
working men were on the whole opposed to restriction;
in 1893 they were largely in favour of it. A demonstra-
tion called by "the trade" at Trafalgar Square against
the Bill was swamped by friends of it, who carried resolu-
tions by overwhelming majorities in its favour. The
change of attitude of the working classes is very likely
partly due to political partisanship; but still it is a notable fact, and makes the way for temperance reform
much smoother than it otherwise would have been.

Owing to the time taken up by the debate on the
Home Rule Bill, the Government found it impossible
to do more than introduce its local option measure in
1893. It promised to proceed with it this Session (1894);
but at the time of writing it seems very improbable that
this will be done.

CHAPTER III.

THE PROBLEMS OF REFORM.

FOUR main problems have to be faced before any adequate scheme of licensing reform can be formulated. They are : (1) compensation ; (2) of whom shall the licensing bodies consist? (3) what is to be done with the clubs? (4) shall "tied houses" be permitted?

COMPENSATION.—This has been for many years the main block to reform. Are publicans, when deprived of their licences through no fault of their own, entitled to compensation or not? For long there was considerable doubt as to the legal aspects of the matter. One party argued that as the publican has his licence granted for one year alone, and as the magistrates have power to refuse to renew such a licence, therefore the drink seller has no vested interest in its continuance, nor the slightest claim to compensation if its renewal is refused. On the other hand, it was said that while the justices have nominally the power of refusing the renewal of old licences, it is a strictly limited power that they never put into force except for wrong-doing on the part of the licensees ; and that the custom has so long prevailed of regularly renewing the certificates of all publicans who behave properly, that an expectation of renewal has become universal ; and

(169)

that by virtue of custom they have a vested interest, and are entitled to compensation if renewal is refused.

The legal aspects of the matter were finally cleared up in 1891 by the decision of the House of Lords in the well-known case of "Sharp *v.* Wakefield". The magistrates of the Kendal division of Westmoreland refused, in September, 1887, to renew the licence of an inn at Kentmere on the grounds of the remoteness of the premises from police supervision, and the character and necessities of the locality. The owner of the house, Susannah Sharp, appealed to the Quarter Sessions, but that body upheld the magistrates. It was resolved by the drink interest to make this case a test one. Their argument was that for the renewal of an existing licence the justices are not entitled to inquire into the character and wants of the neighbourhood, or to refuse a licence on the grounds that there is no longer a necessity for a licensed house there.

The case was taken from court to court, and everywhere the decision of the magistrates was upheld. Finally it came before the House of Lords in January, 1891 ; and the judgment of their lordships was given in the following March. The five law-lords were unanimously of opinion that justices have the right to refuse the renewal of a licence if the circumstances of the neighbourhood or any other sufficient cause render it desirable. The Legislature, their lordships stated, gave the magistrates an absolute discretion both for granting and renewing licences : and such discretion is to be exercised (to quote the Lord Chancellor) "according to the rules of reason and justice, within the limits to which an honest man, competent to the discharge of his office, ought to confine himself".

This decision was a serious blow to the owners of licensed premises. It at once and for ever swept away all claims of a legal right to compensation, and showed that vested interests in licences are absolutely non-existent.

But the question still remains whether, although the publican has no legal claim to compensation, he is not morally entitled (under ordinary circumstances) to some consideration, if suddenly and through no fault of his own he is deprived of what he was for long encouraged to look upon as his right. It is felt by many that it would be a hardship to take from a well-behaved licensed victualler his means of livelihood without some consideration. Whether this sentiment is right or not the writer of this book does not propose to discuss; but it undoubtedly exists, and the temperance party will gain nothing by shutting its eyes to it.

On the one hand we have the claim of prohibitionists that no publican should have a penny from public funds as recompense for dispossession; on the other hand, there is the plea of the "trade" advocates, that he ought to have the full difference between the "trade" value of his house and its value as ordinary premises. The first of these seems rather harsh, and the second is certainly unreasonable. Is there no *via media*?

The unreasonableness of the second proposition may best be seen from the fact that in many towns a very large proportion of the public-houses do not pay their way. Yet every one of these places is valued at a price far above its value as an ordinary business house; consequently, if the authorities were to pay the terms asked by the owners on closing them, they would actually be giving considerable sums for losing concerns.

It may be asked why, if such houses do not clear their expenses, their proprietors keep them open year after year. The reasons are twofold: First, the houses are usually owned by brewers, who fear that if they abandon the licences, rival brewers may persuade the magistrates to grant additional licences in other parts of the place. Secondly, the establishments are often used as traps for depriving the inexperienced of their stock of money. The process is very simple. A house owned by a brewer goes to the bad, custom falls off, and the receipts fail to cover the outgoings. Thereupon the tenant is given notice to quit; and a salaried manager, skilled in the art of drawing custom, is placed in charge of it. This manager is usually a man well known in the neighbourhood, and with plenty of friends. He belongs to nearly all the friendly societies in the place, Buffaloes, Oddfellows, and the rest; he can give a tip on the coming race with any man, and he is "hail fellow, well met" with every Tom, Dick and Harry. All his friends, of course, flock to patronise him; the brewer is careful to supply specially good drink; a pull over is given for every one's measure;

and soon the takings of the house are increased enormously. Then the place is advertised, and a novice is
attracted by it. The brewer's agent shows him the
books, and is able to prove that the business is going up
by leaps and bounds; and so the novice is persuaded to
pay, say £100 in cash for the good-will, and take over
the house. The manager who has drawn all the custom
leaves; and his friends leave with him. The poor new
publican soon finds that he is losing money every week,
and before long he begins to get in debt to the brewer.
This goes on until his debt amounts to the price he paid
for the good-will. Then the agent visits him, explains
that as he is evidently not suited for the trade he had
better go. The brewer will kindly allow the £100 paid
as good-will to go to cancel the debt; and the tenant
must leave as quickly as possible. The house is then
used for the fleecing of another novice; and so on.

If any reader doubts the truth of this, let him consult
some experienced publican who is not afraid to speak
the truth, or let him notice in any moderate-sized town
how often many of the smaller licensed houses are advertised as being "under new management".

Now, it cannot be said that the owners of such houses
as these mentioned have the slightest equitable claim to
any consideration. The only way to avoid paying money
to such would be to base any scheme of pecuniary compensation *not on the artificial trade value of the house, but on the
actual profits gained*, as shown by the books and vouchers
of the place and by the publican's income-tax returns.

A second limit to any scheme of compensation should be that no one, save the licence holder himself, should be entitled to any consideration.   Big brewing firms that have bought up large numbers of licences are well acquainted with the risks attaching to them.   The British public may be anxious to treat the poor licensed victualler generously ; but it will hardly sanction the appropriation by wealthy wholesale firms, that thrive by fostering public misery, of large sums of public money.   This is the opinion of many by no means opposed to any compensation. Mr. Gladstone, in the House of Commons (15th May, 1890), in speaking of this matter, declared : " This I must say, I cannot conceive any state of things in which the State authority would have the smallest duty or the smallest warrant for looking to anybody in these transactions, except the man with whom it deals—that is to say, the man to whom the licence is issued, and on whom it imposes its responsibility ".

In any plan of compensation the money should be raised from the publicans themselves.   Those remaining benefit by the closing of other houses ; for there are fewer shops selling drink, and therefore those left get more custom.   This has already been done successfully in Victoria by means of increased licence fees, etc.

As the publicans have no legal claim to consideration it cannot be expected that any scheme for their compensation will be permanent.   It will rather provide for a softening to them of a time of transition.

Within these limits, surely some practicable scheme

can be formulated. The following, while dealing liberally with the keepers of licensed houses, would yet be an advance on the present position. Let it be arranged that for ten years the men at present holding licences shall be allowed to retain them; and if during those years the authorities wish to close any public-houses they shall pay the holders compensation based on the following scale: during the first two years, five years' purchase, reckoned on the average profits of the previous three years; during the third and fourth years, four years' profits; during the fifth and sixth years, three years' profits, and so on till at the end of the tenth year no compensation would be payable. The funds for such payments to be raised by increased licensing fees and an extra tax on liquor. No money to be paid to any person but the licence holder himself. At the end of the ten years the number of houses could be reduced to a fixed scale, say one for every 500 or 1000 of population.

The principal objectors to such a compromise would probably be the teetotalers. But they would do well to consider whether it will not hasten forward the coming of that sober England for which we all long if some method can be found of breaking through the present intolerable deadlock. There is nothing opposed to temperance in granting compensation. It is merely a matter of policy, not of principle: though, to hear some reformers talk, it might be imagined that the idea of partly recompensing licence holders for their loss involves some terrible wrong.

Both Sir Wilfrid Lawson and Mr. Caine have in the past admitted that a compromise about compensation might be worth considering. In the House of Commons (5th March, 1880) Sir W. Lawson said: " Honourable members tell me that there ought to be something about compensation in my resolution. If I would only do that they would find it in their hearts to vote for me. Now I do not want to condemn compensation, but this is not the question which is before the House. The question is, whether it is right to force these houses upon an unwilling neighbourhood; and if it cannot be done without compensation, let us have compensation. I am very sure that if ever my resolution is crystallised into an Act of Parliament this House will never refuse a fair demand from any body of men."

Mr. Caine, in talking to a *Pall Mall Gazette* interviewer, said, when dealing with the compensation proposals of the Church Temperance Society: " The time plan would work in this way: You might give to all old licences a definite lease of life, ten years being the utmost limit conceivable. . . . At the close of the ten years' term licences would be granted for one year only, and no compensation whatever would be granted in case of extinction. . . . (It) would present to temperance reformers the attractive and important feature of finality. It certainly demands most careful consideration on all hands."

Mr. Chamberlain, in 1876, proposed terms very similar to these. His idea, when discussing the buying up of licensed premises in order to commence municipal public-houses, was that compensation should be paid to the licence holder alone at the rate of five years' profit, based on the average profits of the previous three years.

Truth compels the admission, however, that Mr. Chamberlain's views on this point have greatly altered in recent years. In writing to me in April, 1894, he said :—" Further consideration has convinced me that the method of compensation proposed by me in 1876 would not be the best guide to a fair settlement, and that it would be impossible to ignore the interests of other persons besides the licensed holder. I think now that the best way would be to submit all claims to an official arbitrator, who would be instructed to give for the property such sum as would be given by a willing buyer to a willing seller in the open market—in other words, the fair market price."

LICENSING BODIES.—Of whom should the licensing bodies consist ? There are three different kinds of bodies proposed : (*a*) The magistrates, as at present ; (*b*) county and town councils ; (*c*) elective boards *ad hoc.* The magistrates have for long carried out the necessary duties ; and in the country parts they have done as well as could be expected. In towns, more particularly in small boroughs, their rule has not worked quite so satisfactorily. Occasional charges of being influenced by pecuniary considerations in the performance of their duties have been brought against them ; but such charges are so very rare that direct bribery may be said to be practically unknown. But magistrates in small boroughs are often influenced by some very extra-judicial considerations. Many of them are small tradesmen, appointed for political reasons. They are well acquainted with the brewer who is at the back of the application for a licence, and possibly have business transactions with him : naturally they do not care to offend him, and so a licence is often granted when it ought not to be.

The licensing authority is altogether outside the usual province of the magistrate's duties, which should be purely judicial. It has never been found satisfactory to unite judicial and executive functions in one body ; and jurists are agreed that this should be avoided ; yet while they are the licensing authority the magistrates are both administrators and judges. But the principal objection to magistrates is that they are not in the least representative, and can do as they please entirely irrespective of the public.

A proposal favoured by many statesmen is that of taking the duty of issuing licences from the magistrates and placing it in the hands of county and borough councils. A representative body would thus be secured; but the result of this would simply be to ruin many of the councils. The liquor question would swallow up every other in public estimation, like a veritable Joseph's rod. Men would be elected solely because of their views on licensing reform. The publicans would appoint their candidates, and the teetotalers theirs ; and both parties would have a pitched battle at almost every election. Many good administrators, rather than face such contests, would remain outside, and the whole tone of the councils would be lowered.

The most practicable plan of securing a popular licensing authority seems to be the election of Boards specially for this one purpose, as School Boards are elected for the management of elementary schools. The area which such Boards control should not be too small and particular care would have to be taken to prevent those pecuniarily interested in the traffic getting on them.

But it must be remembered that no change in the *personnel* of the licensing authority will effect much, and it is possible that any change may do harm. A representative body will be more liable to be influenced by outside consideration than are the justices; and the Boards in some places will favour the drink sellers more than the magistrates do now. This consideration has induced some reformers to advocate leaving the administration in the hands of the present authorities, but limiting their power by a direct popular control over the issuance of new licences.

CLUBS.—No licensing reform, however complete the restraints it places on public-houses, will accomplish much unless at the same time it deals with the club evil. In the ordinary drinking club we have something far more dangerous to society than the worst-conducted public-house. Reformers were for long so absorbed in fighting the open drink shop, that they had no time for

attending to anything else; and statesmen of all parties
dreaded arousing against themselves the opposition
which they knew would follow the curtailing of any of
the privileges of club-land. The result is that there is
to-day in every large town a considerable and rapidly
increasing number of drinking dens, subject to no
control, paying no fees, requiring no licences, and
allowed to keep open all day and every day, Sunday and
week-day alike. With the genuine club no one wishes
to meddle; but the majority of places which go under
this name are nothing but drinking and gambling hells,
and are usually financed by, and run for the profit of,
some brewer. Within ten years their number has increased almost tenfold, and from all parts of the land
comes the same tale of the mischief they are doing. Some
months ago, the Dublin Corporation sent a petition to
the Government in which it said: "We view with
alarm and dismay the rapid increase of bogus drinking
clubs in all parts of the city; in our opinion these clubs
are a prolific source of poverty, crime, and disorder;
they are instrumental in depreciating the ratable value
of property wherever they are established; and the laws
which allow, without let or hindrance, their degrading
operations at all hours of the night and of the day, are a
disgrace to civilisation." The Corporation urged the
Government to introduce a measure "that will be effective in grappling with this degrading and pestiferous
evil". At Cardiff the notorious "Field Clubs," formed
solely and avowedly for the purpose of supplying their

members with ale on Sundays, and so setting the Sunday Closing Act at defiance, were able to carry on business for some time without any hindrance from the police. A case which shows even more clearly than this how our licensing system is being reduced to little better than a mere farce, was mentioned last year in the House of Commons. The licence of a certain village public-house had been taken away because of the misconduct of the publican, and because the place was not required. Thereupon the brewer who owned the building opened it as a club, making the former publican manager. The rules were carefully drawn up, with the aid of counsel, to keep the house open to as many as possible; an entrance fee of a few pence was fixed; and the club was in a position to accommodate almost all its old customers. It had not to observe any of the regulations imposed on the regular drink shops, and consequently did twice as much business as before its licence was taken away.

Such instances might be multiplied indefinitely, but there is no need ; for to all who know anything of the inner life of our great cities these things are commonplaces. How to deal with these bogus establishments, and yet not at the same time to unduly interfere with genuine clubs, has become an urgent and serious question. The Royal Commission on the Sunday Closing (Wales) Act recommended that all clubs where intoxicating liquors are sold should be registered with the local authority, and that the register should be open for the inspection of the police. The Commission was also strongly of opinion that "clubs which exist only for the purpose of supplying drink, or only colourably for some other purpose, should be declared absolutely illegal". When Lord Randolph Churchill brought his licensing scheme before the House of Commons, he incorporated with it clauses for the registration and taxation of clubs, as has already been described in the previous chapter. The Bishop of London's Bill in 1893 contained similar clauses, but neither measure ever got beyond the initial stages. *The Clubs Registration Bill*, as amended by a Select Committee of the House of Commons last year, provided (1) that every club (with certain strictly defined exceptions) selling intoxicating liquors on unlicensed premises must be registered; (2) that it shall only be managed in accordance with its registered constitution; and (3) that an annual return shall be made of the members of the club. There were further provisions forbidding the sale of any drink to be taken from the club premises, preventing any person under eighteen years old becoming a member of the club, and limiting the number of honorary members to one for every twenty ordinary members. The Bill applied only to England, and was admitted by its supporters to be miserably inadequate; but it would have been a great improvement, had it passed into law, on the present state of affairs. However, it went the usual way of Bills in that barren Session.

Happily our colonies can teach us something on this matter. During the last nine years there has been an extremely simple yet very practical clause in the Victorian licensing law dealing with clubs. It provides that every *bonâ-fide* association that was formed before the passing of the Act should be regarded as a club ; but that any club established afterwards must, in order to obtain the right to supply its members with intoxicants, consist of "not less than fifty members, united for the purpose of providing accommodation for and conferring privileges and advantages upon the members thereof". Such accommodation has to be provided from the funds of the club, and no person is allowed to get any benefit from the club which may not be shared equally by every member. All clubs have to be registered, and their certificates may be withdrawn at any time by the Licensing Board.

In the Licensed Victuallers' Amendment Act, brought before the South Australian Parliament in 1890, more elaborate provisions were made for meeting the club difficulty. Clubs numbering not less than fifty members in Adelaide, or not less than twenty-five in other parts, are exempt from the ordinary Licensing Act, so far as selling to their own members goes, provided the following conditions exist :—

1. The club must be established upon premises of which such association or company are the *bonâ-fide* occupiers, and maintained from the joint funds of the club ; and no persons must be entitled under its rules to derive any benefit or profit from the club or for the sale of liquors which is not shared equally by every other member.

2. It must have been proved to the satisfaction of the licensing bench at an annual or quarterly meeting that the club is such an association or company as in this section is defined, and that the premises of the club are suitable for the purpose.

3. It must be proved to the satisfaction of the licensing bench that such club has a committee of management, and that some person has been appointed by them steward or manager.

The club is obliged to pay an annual registration fee of £5, and to obtain a certificate from the clerk of the licensing district; such certificate being withdrawable if any of the conditions under which it is issued are broken.

On some such lines as these we must look for the solution of the club problem in England. Any measure to be really effective must provide, first, that proprietary clubs and clubs financed by those interested in the sale of drink shall be treated exactly the same as public-houses. The various regulations given in *The Clubs Registration Bill* should be retained, but the certificate of registration should only be obtainable after the licensing justices are satisfied as to the genuine character of the association, and have ascertained that it is established primarily for some other purpose than the supply of intoxicants. As clubs cause a decided diminution in the revenue obtained from licensed houses, it seems reasonable that they should be subject to a special excise tax, graduated somewhat after the manner provided in Lord Randolph Churchill's Bill.

TIED HOUSES.—During recent years it has become
more and more common for brewers to own public-houses,
and to make the holders of the licences nominees of their
own, dismissable at will.   In many towns over four-fifths
of the drink shops are either owned or controlled by
brewers or wholesale spirit merchants.   Year by year
the wholesale firms are driven by competition to purchase
more and more houses; and soon it will be difficult to
find establishments in which the nominal publican is
master of his own business.   It was manifestly the intention of Parliament, in passing the various licensing Acts,
to make the managers of licensed houses responsible
persons, who would have some stake in the business,
and to whose interest it would be to strictly observe
the law; but by the "tied-house" system all this is
changed.   Through it the licensee is but little better than
a man of straw, and the real controller is the brewer.

There are two principal ways in which the wholesale
firms "tie" a house.   The first is as follows: A man
with a small amount of capital wishes to take a public-
house.   The price of the good-will, stock and fittings of
the place is, say, £1500.   The would-be publican has
only £300, but a brewer agrees to lend him £800, and
a spirit merchant £400, on condition that he binds
himself to deal solely off them for his liquors.   This
is the least objectionable method.   The other way is for
the brewer to be the owner of the public-house, and the
publican his tenant.   The latter pays a certain amount,
varying according to the value of the house, as good-will;

and it is stipulated that he shall deal off the brewer for all his malt liquors. He is usually liable to dismissal at a very short notice ; and it is an understood thing that if the trade of the house drops at all he will have to leave. He must push his business at any cost and by any means. Most of the breaches of the law committed by publicans are due to this ; for the unhappy licensed victualler has often no choice except between fostering his trade by illegal methods or getting notice to quit.

It might be thought that it is hardly to the interest of the brewers to risk losing the licences in order to do a somewhat larger trade ; but those who argue thus are not acquainted with the working of the law. Let us suppose a case typical of many. A publican is convicted before the magistrates on some very serious charge, say that of harbouring improper characters ; and his licence is endorsed. It may be mentioned, in passing, that most magistrates refuse to endorse a licence except an offence is very grave or frequently repeated. At the next licensing sessions the case comes on, and the justices demur at renewing the certificate. The lawyer for the owners then addresses them somewhat in this way. " The house in question," he says, " is owned by the well-known firm of Messrs. Grey & Black. They had not the slightest idea that their tenant was guilty of such conduct as was unhappily proved, and they greatly regret it. It is their wish to keep their houses respectable, and they do all in their power to accomplish this. In this case, immediately the licence holder was con-

victed they gave him notice to quit. The good-will of
the house has been sold to Mr. Tom Brown for a
substantial consideration, and the old tenant who was
convicted has no longer any interest in the place. Mr.
Brown is a *most* respectable man ; and I can bring forward unimpeachable witnesses, gentlemen well known
to you, who will testify to this fact. Now, gentlemen,
I cannot deny that you have the power to refuse the
licence if you wish ; but I would venture to point out to
you that by doing so you would punish, not the man
whose wrongdoing we all condemn, but Messrs. Grey &
Black who own the premises, and Mr. Tom Brown who
has bought the good-will. Mr. Brown, though he has
done nothing wrong, will be the loser of a very considerable sum by such a refusal. You will, perhaps, permit
me to say, gentlemen, with all deference to your judgment, that such a course would not be in accordance
with justice, nor with the honourable traditions that have
always distinguished this bench."

In nineteen cases out of twenty the magistrates agree
that it would be rather hard on Brown to refuse ; and accordingly they grant the renewal. The risks of losing a
licence are so small that they are hardly worth taking into
consideration. First of all, there is very little probability
of the police proceeding against a house, except when compelled by outside pressure. Then, when the police do proceed and secure a conviction, the licence is not usually
endorsed. Even after endorsement, a judicious change
of tenants can be made ; and so the licence retained.

The system of "tied houses" is bad for every one except the brewer. It is bad for the publican, for it reduces him from master of his own house to a servant of the wholesale firms. He has to take such liquor as they please, and pay the price they demand for it. It is a recognised custom in the trade for some if not all of the brewers to charge their "tied" customers more than they do the free.

The plan is bad for the public. In place of the main business of the publican being to satisfy his customers, it is to retain the good-will of the owner of the house. In a district where one firm controls all the houses, there is no longer competition between the different publicans as to which shall sell the best drink, for all sell the same; and the brewer is able to palm off his worst brews on the people there.

Last, but chief of all, it is bad for good order and for the general well-being. The licensed victualler, being placed in such a position, is too often willing to adopt risky methods for attracting custom, which he would not venture to employ had he a substantial stake in the house. By this he not only injures the character of his own premises, but compels his rivals, who own free houses, to imitate him in order that they may not lose their trade. And so the whole method of conducting business in the neighbourhood is lowered.

The *Times* cannot be accused of teetotal bias; and an utterance by it on this matter will command weight. "The natural tendency of a brewer is simply to push the sale of his beer," said that journal in a leading article on 12th September, 1892. "Provided no forfeiture of the licence be incurred, the especial manner in which the business is conducted does not matter much to him. His main desire is that the neighbourhood shall drink as much as possible. His servant, the publican, who has little or no property invested in the premises, has no strong personal motive for caution. He wishes to ingratiate himself with his employer by promoting a liberal consumption. The fear of risking the licence affects him far less than if it meant for him positive commercial ruin. From the point of view even of the customers, it has been felt that a spread of the monopoly of brewers is inconvenient. When a brewer is absolute master of a house he can, unchallenged, supply it with bad or unwholesome liquors. . . . Practical experience, at all events, has created a keen jealousy of the system of tied houses, and a determination to make a stand against its unlimited predominance. . . . Where the function of a court is the commission to certain persons to conduct a trade under its supervision, its manifest duty is to see that its delegates are free agents. A publican who can be ejected at once, or be subjected to ruinous penalties, if he exercise the least liberty of choice of his stock, and unless he accept any trash a brewer consigns to him, is a cipher."

A remedy lies all ready in the hands of the licensing justices, if they would only use it. Nothing would be easier than for them to demand the production of all agreements under which the publicans are occupiers of their houses, and to refuse (after due notice) to grant the renewal of the licence of any house in which the tenant is not a *bonâ-fide* free agent. But there is little prospect of the licensing justices doing this until they are compelled. The most practicable remedy seems to be a short Act of Parliament, providing that in no case is a licensed victualler to enter into any contracts which will make him responsible to any but the licensing authority for the conduct of his house ; and that it shall be illegal for him to bind himself to purchase his stock in whole or part from any particular firm or firms. It should be forbidden for brewers or wholesale spirit merchants to own all or part of any public-houses. It might be further provided that the licensing authority is to satisfy itself that the publican is genuinely a free agent before granting or renewing his licence.

Such an Act would no doubt receive considerable opposition from many brewers, though even to some of them it would not be unwelcome. The present method compels them to sink a vast amount of capital in buying up licences, and gives the small brewer (who possibly produces better drink than his wealthier rivals) little chance of competing against the great firms. To the majority of publicans such a law would be acceptable, for it would raise their position and increase their profits. And the gain to public order would be greater than that which is likely to result from many more ambitious schemes.

CHAPTER IV.

THE PATH OF PROGRESS.

THE problem of licensing reform, as every one who has given it even the most cursory attention will readily admit, is by no means an easy one. Whatever step may be proposed is certain to excite the opposition of many. It is impossible for even the most astute statesman to formulate a plan that will receive the assent and approval of extremists of either school. Almost every one, Liberal or Conservative, admits that the present state of affairs is wholly unsatisfactory, and that it demands immediate treatment. Under it we have a vastly excessive number of public-houses, a weak system of supervision, and an entire lack of local control. The publican who wishes to carry on his business decently and respectably often finds it impossible to do so without heavy pecuniary sacrifice, on account of his more unscrupulous licensed rivals, who are willing to descend to any tricks to increase their trade. The whole system of licensing is based on the personal caprices of individual magistrates rather than on any uniform plan.

For many years all these things have been admitted and deplored. For at least a quarter of a century statesmen have declared that the present state of the law is disgraceful, and cannot be permitted to longer continue. Yet it still remains the same.

Can nothing be done? Are the imagined interests of a small body of rich men to over-ride the welfare of the whole nation? It almost seems as though our legislators had resigned themselves to this. One thing at least is certain. No sweeping change has any hope, at least for the present, of coming into law. A drastic licensing Bill, into which one of the great political parties put all its strength, might pass the House of Commons, but would inevitably be defeated by the Lords. The body which rejected without a division the Bishop of London's Bill, and which mutilated the non-partisan Irish Sale of Intoxicating Liquors Bill, will show but little consideration for any thorough-going schemes. Reformers of one school reply: "Then let us abolish the House of Lords". This is very easy to say; but if we have to wait for licensing reform until the Lords are abolished, then there is not much hope for improvement in this generation. A more politic course would seem to be the carrying of temperance legislation by piecemeal. Little by little the law may be changed; glaring anomalies may be removed, manifest injustices altered, until at last, while our liquor laws will not be theoretically perfect, they may at least be made reasonably workable.

The following suggestions as to the lines which such alterations might take contain nothing that has not been approved by many members of Parliament of both parties.

1. It is generally admitted that there are far too many

public-houses. No doubt it would be found very difficult to reduce the number of those already licensed, but
there should be little trouble in preventing the issuance
of new licences. Let it be enacted that in no case shall
a person be permitted to apply for a public-house licence
unless he has previously obtained the signatures of one
half of the resident electors in the immediate neighbourhood to a petition requesting such a licence. Even when
such signatures have been obtained, the magistrates would
still retain their option of refusal.

2. The second reform has already been before the
House of Commons. Let every district have the option
of Sunday closing, as provided in the *Liquor Traffic
(Local Control) Bill,* 1893. To this might well be added
the choice of keeping the houses open on Sundays for
two hours only.

3. Let the appeal to Quarter Sessions in case of the
refusal of the renewal of licences be abolished, except
for manifest illegality on the part of the local licensing
session. At present the licensing magistrates in many
parts will not use their unquestioned power of refusing
unnecessary licences, because they are aware that their
decision is almost certain to be reversed at the Quarter
Sessions. The county magistrates, knowing nothing of
local needs, continually over-ride the deliberate judgment
of the local justices.

4. Have a system of supervision of public-houses entirely independent of local control, as proposed by Mr.
Bruce in 1871.

Those who have carefully watched the working of the present laws know that the police do no part of their work so inefficiently as the control of public-houses. This is due to two causes—bribery, and the power of the drink sellers in local government. The bribes received by the police are usually very small, and no doubt many constables look upon them as their regular perquisites. The man on the beat knows where he will find a pot of beer left out for him on a hot day ; and he would be more than human if he did not look on the doings of the publican with a kindly eye after quenching his thirst with the publican's liquor. But this securing the good-will of the police is comparatively unimportant, and is practically incapable of legal proof. A far more serious thing is the influence steadily brought to bear on the police in many small municipalities, to cause them to refrain from proceeding against certain public-houses. The municipal police are solely dependent for pay and promotion on the Local Watch Committee and the Town Council. The Council is often largely controlled by the men who own the public-houses. Now the most obtuse policeman well understands that if he were to lay information against the manager of a house owned by a town councillor, or by the head of one of the local political associations, it would make his prospects of advancement no brighter. He might be praised by the papers for his zeal ; but when a chance of promotion came up, he would be passed over for some one else.

This is no imaginary danger. Many who have tried

to secure the better enforcement of licensing laws in towns know well that too often the police will not move further than they are compelled, and then they will do as little as is compatible with appearances.

If there were public-house inspectors entirely independent of local influence, and frequently moved from place to place, a great improvement in the management of many licensed premises would at once be apparent. The law-abiding publican would have a better chance of success, and would not be handicapped in the way he is at present.

5. Let all public-houses be closed on municipal and parliamentary election days.

Other urgently needed reforms, such as the control of clubs, and the abolition of tied houses, have been described in preceding chapters, and need not be recapitulated here.

* * * * * * * * * *

I feel that I would be untrue to my own convictions if I closed this volume without a final word to those who have followed me so far. I have tried to treat the subject calmly and dispassionately; and zealous reformers may possibly complain (as some have already complained of those parts published in periodical form) that my tone is cold and unsympathetic. I can only assure them that it is from no lack of earnest desire to promote true temperance. But the cause of reform will not be advanced by special pleading, or by that impetuous enthusiasm which leads men to overlook facts in

order to give a reasonable air to their theories. The
first work of a reformer should be to master his facts,
and to discover what lessons the experiments and the
mistakes of those who have preceded him can teach.

We are often told that it is impossible to make men
sober by Act of Parliament; and no doubt all legislation
that seeks to suppress evil has to fight against strong
opposition. But do those who so lightly quote this empty
aphorism ever seriously resolve to persuade men to be
sober by other means? or are they content to let a smart
phrase run glibly from their lips as an excuse for doing
nothing? To-day we are face to face with a gigantic evil
that is destroying much that is brightest and fairest in our
national life. To all who have any notion of patriotism,
to all who have any real desire for the welfare of the
people, and especially to all to whom the commands of
the Carpenter of Nazareth are something more than mere
words,—the call comes to take their part in the battle for
its suppression. How are we to work, each man must
decide for himself; but none of us can shirk the manifest
duty of doing something, and of doing our best, without
wrong.

It is admitted that Acts of Parliament can help in promoting sobriety only so far as they are backed up by a
strong public sentiment, and by the earnest endeavours of
the people. Legislation can remove temptation, it can
make virtue easier; but it cannot do everything. Along
with it must go steady work for the brightening of every-
day life, for the easing of conditions of labour, for im-

proving the dwellings of the poor, for raising the moral tone, for the realisation by all of the sacredness of this life, and the need to make the most of its opportunities.

As we survey the forces against us in this fight, we may sometimes be inclined to despair of its issue. On the side of intemperance and self-indulgence are great resources of wealth, power, self-interest, and unscrupulousness. Shall we conquer, or is the wrong to triumph over us? The words of a great thinker, written on another subject, best give the answer: "The ultimate issue of the struggle is certain. If any one doubts the general preponderance of good over evil in human nature, he has only to study the history of moral crusades. The enthusiastic energy and self-devotion with which a great moral cause inspires its soldiers always have prevailed, and always will prevail, over any amount of self-interest or material power arrayed on the other side."[1]

[1] Mr. Goldwin Smith.

APPENDIX I.

THE CONDITION OF WORKING MEN IN MAINE.

THE *Fifth Annual Report of the Bureau of Industrial and Labour Statistics for Maine* (Augusta, 1892) gives a set of very full returns from which it is possible to ascertain the exact position of working men under prohibition. A personal canvass was made of working men of all classes, the unskilled and lower paid, as well as the best and highest paid. Space will not permit me to quote more than a brief *résumé*.

" The following is a general summary of some of the more important statistics derived from the reports of working men. Whole number of reports, 1082; number American born, 895; number foreign born, 187; number owning homes, 285; value of homes, 405,850 dollars; number of homes mortgaged, 60; amount of mortgages, 26,169 dollars; number renting, 481; number having savings bank accounts, 181; number who have accumulated savings in former years, 696; during past year, 595; run into debt during past year, 104; neither gained nor lost during past year, 383."

Of 745 men with families, the average annual income was 527 dollars 1 cent per family yearly. The average annual income of 265 single working men was 395 dollars 1 cent, and of 53 single working women, 259 dollars 64 cents. The amounts saved from income averaged, men with families, 12 per cent., single men, 17 per cent., and single women, 9 per cent.

APPENDIX II.

THE GIN ACT, 1736.

WHEREAS the excessive drinking of spirituous liquors by the common people tends not only to the destruction of their health, and the debauching of their morals, but to public ruin:

For remedy thereof—

Be it enacted, that from the 29th September no person shall presume, by themselves or any others employed by them, to sell or retail any brandy, rum, arrack, usquebaugh, geneva, aqua vitæ, or any other distilled spirituous liquors, mixed or unmixed, in any less quantity than two gallons, without first taking out a licence for that purpose within ten days at least before they sell or retail the same; for which they shall pay down £50, to be renewed ten days before the year expires, paying the like sum; and in case of neglect to forfeit £100; such licences to be taken out within the limits of the penny post at the chief office of excise, London, and at the next chief office of excise for the country. And be it enacted, that for all such spirituous liquors as any retailers shall be possessed of on or after the 29th September, 1736, there shall be paid a duty of 20s. per gallon, and so on in proportion for a greater or lesser quantity above all other duties charged on the same.

The collecting the rates by this Act imposed to be under the management of the commissioners and officers of excise by all the excise laws now in force (except otherwise provided by this Act); and all monies arising by the said duties or licences for sale thereof shall be paid into the receipt of his majesty's exchequer, distinctly from other branches of the public revenue; one moiety of the fines, penalties and forfeitures to be paid to his majesty and successors, the other to the person who shall inform on any one for the same.

www.ingramcontent.com/pod-product-compliance
Lightning Source LLC
Chambersburg PA
CBHW030832270326
41928CB00007B/1014